Retreat Riches

Revitalize Any Business with Strategic Getaways

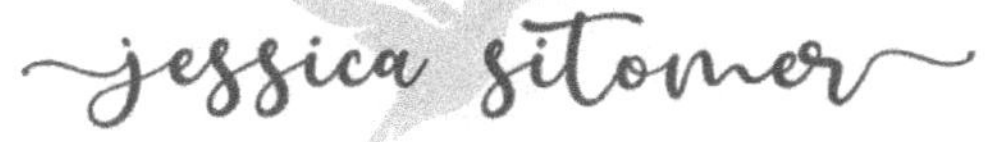

No part of this publication may be reproduced, stored in retrieval systems, or transmitted in any form or by any means, electronic, mechanical, photocopying, recording, or otherwise, without express permission of the publisher, except where indicated.

First edition 2024

For more information about Jessica, please visit:
JessicaSitomer.com

TABLE OF CONTENTS

INTRODUCTION

In a serene setting, away from the hustle and bustle of daily life, a group of individuals gathers, each one on their personal quest for growth, understanding, and transformation. The air is filled with anticipation, a sense of camaraderie, and an undeniable energy that promises change. As the retreat unfolds, deep connections are forged, perspectives shift, and both the host and participants emerge profoundly transformed. This isn't a fleeting moment; it's a pivotal experience that reshapes careers, reignites passion, and redefines personal and professional paths.

I'm Jessica Sitomer, your guide on creating this type of transformative journey. With a background steeped in driving growth and career success as a Vice President of Training, I've navigated the waters of change, faced the challenges of building meaningful connections, and celebrated the victories of breakthrough moments. My journey has led me to become a 3-time Best Selling Author and a sought-after Keynote Speaker dedicated to empowering entrepreneurs and small business owners like you to thrive. My passion lies in creating spaces for transformation—experiential retreats that offer more than just an escape but a doorway to deeper relationships, personal growth, and business success.

This book is a testament to that passion. It's crafted for Coaches, Facilitators, Speakers, Counselors, Writers & Artists, and Influencers like yoga teachers, health and wellness coaches, marriage counselors, writing coaches, business mentors, healers, and creators of all kinds who seek to deepen their impact through the powerful medium of retreats.

Here, you'll find a unique blend of practical strategies and inspirational stories, all designed to guide you in hosting retreats that not only expand your business but also create lasting bonds and transformative experiences for you and your clientele.

Unlike any other book on this topic, "Retreat Riches: Revitalize Any Business with Strategic Getaways" offers an immersive, step-by-step guide tailored specifically for small businesses and entrepreneurs. Through real-life examples, actionable advice, and a touch of inspiration, this book serves as your comprehensive roadmap to planning, marketing, and executing retreats that resonate deeply with your clients and elevate your business to new heights.

To you, the entrepreneur, the small business owner, the teacher, coach, or instructor with a vision to grow and a desire to connect more meaningfully with your clientele, this book speaks directly to your aspirations. It acknowledges the challenges you face and champions the incredible potential that lies within experiential retreats to transform both your personal and professional life.

My own journey attending retreats was marked by a pivotal moment during my first retreat, which a business coach hosted at Camelback Inn, AZ. The location was so luxurious, exposing me to what was possible for me when I became a successful entrepreneur. The bonding with the other women at the retreat created friendships that have lasted over a decade. Celebrating how far we've come has been a joy. If the event had been held at an airport hotel ballroom, it wouldn't have had half of the power of the retreat.

I sought out other retreats, and the profound impact of genuine, deep connections became undeniably clear. These experiences shape the foundation of this book, lending credibility and a personal touch to the promise of transformation through retreats.

Structured to provide ease of understanding and application, the book unfolds in a series of key parts and chapters that guide you from the conceptualization to the realization of your retreat. Each section builds upon the last, ensuring a seamless journey from inspiration to action.

So, as you turn this page, consider it an invitation to step into a world of possibility. This isn't just about hosting retreats; it's about creating experiences that enrich lives, including your own. Let's embark on this journey together, transforming aspirations into reality and, in doing so, enriching not just our businesses but our very beings. Welcome to "Retreat Riches: Revitalize Any Business with Strategic Getaways."

NOTE TO READER

Before we embark on this journey together, I want to make clear "what's in it for you." As the VP of Training for over 100K Travel Agents, one of my favorite topics to train about is how to find a "Pied Piper." During that training, I taught the Travel Agents why a person of influence would want to create a group retreat. You, the Pied Piper in this case, can look forward to the following when you host a retreat:

1. Many leaders dream of hosting retreats but don't. Isn't that always the way? 90% are dreamers and 10% are doers. After reading this book, you will have all the tools you need to create your first retreat and become part of the 10%, which means you will be perceived as the ultimate expert in your profession.

2. Your access can expand worldwide. If your clients are local, there's a good chance you also market on social media, so you are missing out on all your online followers who want an in-person experience.

3. Customer/client loyalty elevates when they have personal interaction with you during a retreat. The connection you form with attendees is far different than in your place of business.

4. Relationships will be built amongst your attendees creating a community revolving around your content.

5. Your referrals will increase because attendees are going to want to bring friends and families to have an experience.

6. Your list and influence with increase providing opportunities to write a book, create products, guest on podcasts and tv shows, and more.

Dream big because when you think about your ten-year goals, retreats are an impactful way to achieve them faster.

CHAPTER 1
The Importance of Niche in Retreat Planning

In the world of business and personal growth, carving out a unique space where your voice can be distinctly heard is more than a strategic move; it's a necessity. This chapter delves into the critical role that focusing on a niche, plays in the planning and execution of successful retreats. The effectiveness of this approach is not merely theoretical; it's a proven path to creating experiences that resonate deeply with participants, fostering both transformation and community.

When you step into a crowded marketplace, the individuals who stand out are those who speak directly to the needs and desires of a specific group. They don't shout to be heard by everyone; instead, they converse, engaging in a dialogue that feels personal, relevant, and deeply resonant. This principle is the cornerstone of effective retreat planning. By honing in on a niche, you're not limiting your reach; you're amplifying your impact.

Focusing on a niche helps in creating tailored experiences that meet specific needs.

Consider the approach of a seasoned gardener. When planting, they don't scatter seeds indiscriminately across all corners of their garden, hoping something takes root. Instead, they select a specific plot, considering the unique conditions and the type of plant they wish to nurture. This targeted approach ensures that the garden thrives. Similarly, identifying your niche allows you to cultivate an environment where your retreat can flourish. It enables you to tailor the theme, content, and activities to align with the specific interests, challenges, and aspirations of your target audience. This alignment not only increases the relevance of your retreat but also its transformative potential.

Identifying a niche can guide the selection of topics, activities, and guest speakers that align with the interests and needs of the target audience.

The power of a well-defined niche is evident in the realm of wellness retreats. For instance, a retreat focusing on mindfulness for corporate leaders addresses a distinct intersection of needs: stress management, leadership development, and personal growth. By selecting topics such as mindful communication, leadership presence, and resilience and pairing them with activities that promote introspection and relaxation, the retreat speaks directly to the hearts and minds of its participants. Guest speakers are also chosen for their expertise in areas relevant to the niche, providing insights and strategies that participants can apply in their professional and personal lives. This deliberate alignment creates a cohesive, impactful experience that resonates on multiple levels.

Successful case studies of niche retreats demonstrate the effectiveness of targeted planning.

Real-world examples abound of niche retreats that have achieved remarkable success by meeting the nuanced needs of their participants. A retreat designed for writers, focusing on overcoming writer's block through nature-inspired creativity exercises, exemplifies this. By facilitating sessions in serene, natural settings and incorporating activities that stimulate creativity, such as guided walks and journaling beside a tranquil lake, the retreat offers a unique value proposition. The testimonials from attendees, who describe breakthroughs in their writing and renewed inspiration, underscore the potency of a niche-focused approach.

Strategies for researching and selecting a niche based on market demand, personal expertise, and passion are essential.

Selecting the right niche involves a blend of market research, self-reflection, and strategic thinking. Start by exploring areas where there is a clear demand but limited offerings. Social media groups, forums, and existing literature can provide insights into the challenges and desires of potential niches. Equally important is aligning your niche with your areas of expertise and passion. The intersection of what you love, what you're good at, and what people are willing to pay for is where your unique niche likely resides. For example, if you have a background in corporate training and a personal passion for yoga, a retreat focusing on integrating yogic principles into leadership practices could be your niche. This synergy ensures that you bring both knowledge and genuine enthusiasm to the retreat, enhancing its authenticity and appeal.

In sum, the meticulous selection of a niche is not merely a preliminary step in the planning of a retreat; it is the foundation upon which the entire experience is built. By infusing your retreat with a clear focus, you not only enhance its relevance and impact but also create a beacon that attracts individuals who share your values and vision. Through this targeted approach, you're able to offer not just a retreat but a transformational journey that resonates deeply with each participant, fostering both personal growth and a sense of community.

Here are some examples of Niche Retreats:
1. Zen Oasis Retreat: Embrace tranquility and mindfulness through meditation, yoga, and nature immersion.
2. Adventure Quest Retreat: Combine team-building activities, outdoor challenges, and personal growth for an adventurous escape.

3.   Soulful Self-Discovery: Dive deep into self-reflection, journaling, and transformative workshops to discover your inner purpose.

4.   Artistic Expression Escape: Tap into creativity with painting, writing, and other artistic endeavors for a retreat focused on self-expression.

5.   Digital Detox Haven: Unplug and reconnect with nature, yourself, and others, fostering genuine connections without screens.

6.   Wellness Wonderland: Explore holistic well-being with spa treatments, healthy cuisine, and wellness workshops.

7.   Culinary Exploration Retreat: Delight the senses with cooking classes, food tastings, and a focus on mindful eating.

8.   Mindful Leadership Symposium: A retreat tailored for leaders, promoting mindful decision-making, effective communication, and strategic planning.

9.   Eco-Conscious Retreat: Foster environmental awareness through sustainable practices, nature excursions, and eco-friendly workshops.

10.   Community Building Bonanza: Strengthen bonds through team-building activities, shared experiences, and collaborative projects.

11.   Futuristic Innovation Forum: Explore cutting-edge ideas, emerging technologies, and future trends for a forward-thinking retreat.

12.   Healing Through Harmony: Integrate music therapy, sound healing, and rhythm-based activities for a retreat centered on harmony.

13. Mind, Body, Spirit Integration: Align mental, physical, and spiritual well-being through a holistic approach to health.
14. Literary Escape Retreat: Immerse yourself in the world of literature, creative writing, and storytelling for an inspiring retreat.
15. Adaptable Resilience Retreat: Cultivate resilience and adaptability through workshops, challenges, and mindset training.
16. Wilderness Wisdom Weekend: Connect with nature, wildlife, and outdoor survival skills for an adventurous and educational retreat.
17. Global Cultural Exchange: Celebrate diversity with cultural showcases, international cuisine, and cross-cultural dialogues.
18. Mindful Technology Retreat: Find balance in the digital age with workshops on mindful tech use, digital detox practices, and tech-free zones.
19. Fitness Fusion Fiesta: Combine various fitness disciplines, outdoor activities, and wellness practices for a fitness-focused retreat.
20. Dreamscape Vision Quest: Ignite creativity and vision through dream analysis, visualization exercises, and goal-setting activities.

Right now, brainstorm three ideas for retreats that tie into your talent.

Before you continue, I want to give you an option that will take a huge burden off your decision to host a retreat.

Partner with a Travel Agent. Yes, they still exist and are more important now than ever before.

In the realm of hosting impactful retreats, the significance of selecting an ideal location cannot be overstated. It's the backdrop against which the tapestry of your retreat's experiences unfolds. However, the logistics of scouting, securing, and managing the perfect venue can take time and effort. This is where the expertise of a travel agent becomes invaluable. By shifting the burden of location logistics and travel arrangements off your shoulders, you're free to focus on what truly matters—crafting content that transforms and marketing that resonates.

A travel agent brings a world of options to your fingertips, presenting locations you might have yet to consider but that perfectly align with your retreat's theme and objectives. Imagine the possibilities: a serene cruise that offers both the luxury of isolation and the beauty of the sea; all-inclusive resorts where every need of your participants is catered to, allowing them to immerse in the retreat experience fully; a charming farmhouse in Italy where the rustic setting enriches your content with authenticity; or perhaps a wellness spa and resort that adds a layer of rejuvenation to your retreat's offerings. Each location choice, from a villa that offers an intimate setting to a luxury train that takes your participants on a journey through breathtaking landscapes, adds a unique dimension to the retreat experience.

Moreover, the logistical aspects of planning such retreats—

booking airfare for clients, arranging transfers to the venue, and organizing excursions that complement your retreat's theme—can quickly become overwhelming. A travel agent navigates these complexities with ease, ensuring a seamless experience for both you and your participants. They handle the minutiae, from flight schedules to transportation on the ground, allowing you to remain focused on delivering value through your retreat's content and activities.

One of the most compelling reasons to partner with a travel agent lies in the cost-effectiveness of this approach. Many retreat hosts are pleasantly surprised to learn that travel agents often do not charge their fees directly. Instead, they earn commissions from the suppliers (hotels, airlines, resorts, etc.), meaning their expertise and services come at no additional cost to you. Furthermore, their industry connections and negotiating prowess can unlock preferential rates and perks that would be challenging to secure on your own. In some cases, if your group is large enough, these negotiations can even result in complimentary stays for the host.

Travel agents also bring a wealth of knowledge and insight to the table, offering advice that goes beyond simple bookings. Their recommendations are tailored not just to the practicalities of location and logistics but to enhance the overall experience of your retreat. They can suggest venues that align with your retreat's ethos, recommend timing that maximizes the location's appeal, and even advise on local customs or attractions that could enrich your program. Their expertise ensures that the location and logistics of your retreat amplify its impact rather than detract from it.

In essence, the collaboration between a retreat host and a travel agent is symbiotic. While you pour your expertise and passion into developing transformative content and compelling marketing strategies, your travel agent ensures that the stage upon which your retreat unfolds is set to perfection. This partnership not only elevates the quality of the retreat experience but also significantly reduces the stress and workload on you as the host, freeing you to channel your energies where they matter most.

By choosing to work with a travel agent, you're not just outsourcing tasks; you're enhancing the very fabric of your retreat. You're ensuring that every aspect, from the moment participants board their flight to the final day's farewell, is thoughtfully curated and seamlessly executed. This level of professionalism and attention to detail doesn't go unnoticed. It contributes to the overall satisfaction of your participants, encouraging rave reviews, repeat attendance, and word-of-mouth recommendations.

In a landscape where the difference between a good retreat and an unforgettable one often lies in the details, the role of a travel agent is pivotal. They are not just service providers but partners in the truest sense, invested in the success of your retreat and committed to creating an environment where your content can shine, your participants can grow, and your business can flourish. Through this partnership, you're equipped not only to meet the expectations of your participants but to exceed them, setting a new standard for what retreats can achieve.

Now that the weight of travel and destination has been lifted off your shoulders, let's dive into your creativity.

Crafting Your Vision Statement: Beyond the Basics

A vision statement isn't just a collection of words; it's the heartbeat of your retreat. It encapsulates what you aspire to achieve and the transformative journey you intend for your participants. This statement serves as your north star, guiding every decision, from choosing the venue to selecting activities that align with the core essence of your retreat.

The Essence of a Powerful Vision Statement
At its core, a powerful vision statement embodies the essence, values, and overarching objectives of your retreat. It should paint a vivid picture of the experience and its impact on participants, stirring excitement and anticipation. The components of such a vision statement include:

- Clarity: It's direct and straightforward, leaving no room for ambiguity about the retreat's purpose.
- Inspiration: It should inspire not only the potential participants but also you and your team.
- Alignment: It aligns with your values and those of your intended audience, creating a deep resonance.

- Aspiration: It sets a lofty goal, aiming for transformative outcomes that challenge both you and your participants to grow.

Step-by-Step Guide to Crafting Your Vision Statement

Writing a vision statement that captures the spirit of your retreat requires introspection, creativity, and a clear understanding of your goals. Follow this guide to craft a statement that resonates:

1. Brainstorming Session: Start with a brainstorming session focused on the impact you want your retreat to have. Think about the transformations you wish to see in your participants. Consider using mind maps or vision boards to visualize these outcomes.
2. Drafting: Begin drafting your vision statement, keeping it concise yet evocative. Aim for a sentence or two that summarizes the retreat's essence and its impact.
3. Refinement: Refine your draft, focusing on clarity and inspiration. Ensure it speaks directly to the hearts of your target audience, invoking a sense of belonging and anticipation.
4. Feedback Loop: Share your vision statement with peers, mentors, or a select group of your target audience. Gather feedback and be open to revisions that could enhance its clarity and impact.

Templates and Exercises

For those who appreciate a more structured approach, consider using templates and exercises designed to streamline the process. A simple template might look like this:

"Our retreat, [Retreat Name], is dedicated to [Objective/Transformation] by [Method/Activity], in a [Setting], fostering [Outcome]."

Additionally, engage in exercises that prompt deeper reflection:

- Five Whys: Ask yourself "why" five times to drill down to the core purpose of your retreat. This exercise helps uncover the fundamental values and goals driving your vision.
- Participant Perspective: Imagine you are a participant. What would you hope to gain from this retreat? This shift in perspective can bring clarity and empathy to your vision statement.

Incorporating Feedback

Once you have a draft of your vision statement, incorporating feedback is a critical step. This means something other than changing your vision to please everyone but refining it to ensure it resonates as intended. Feedback can come from:

- Potential Attendees: Their insights can reveal whether your vision statement captures the essence and value they seek in a retreat.
- Peers and Mentors: Experienced individuals can offer guidance on clarity and impact, ensuring your vision statement is both aspirational and grounded.

In practice, feedback helps you refine your vision statement from something broad and generic to something specific and compelling. For instance, transforming "Our retreat helps you relax and find peace" to "Our retreat empowers you to master mindfulness techniques, transforming stress into serenity amidst the tranquility of the mountains."

In conclusion, a well-crafted vision statement is more than just a foundational piece of your retreat planning—it's the soul of the experience you're creating. It guides every decision, ensuring that your retreat not only achieves its goals but also resonates deeply with those who embark on the journey with you. Through clarity, inspiration, and alignment, your vision statement becomes a beacon, attracting those who share your aspirations and values and setting the stage for a transformative experience that echoes far beyond the confines of the retreat itself.

Aligning Vision with Audience Needs

The ultimate measure of a retreat's success lies in its resonance with the specific needs and expectations of its intended audience. This alignment is not coincidental but the result of deliberate efforts to understand the audience deeply and adapt the retreat's vision accordingly. This part explores the concrete steps needed to ensure that your retreat not only meets but exceeds the anticipations of your attendees, creating a memorable and transformative experience.

Gathering Insights About Your Target Audience
Understanding your audience begins with active listening and gathering data through various means. Surveys,

interviews, and social media analysis stand out as effective tools for this purpose. Surveys, both online and offline, can yield quantitative and qualitative data about your audience's preferences, challenges, and expectations. Interviews, whether conducted in person or via digital platforms, offer a deeper, more nuanced understanding of individual attendees' needs and aspirations. Social media analysis, on the other hand, provides a broader view of trends, common questions, and discussions within your target audience's community.

- Surveys: Crafting concise, targeted questions that probe into what your audience seeks in a retreat experience. For example, questions could range from logistical preferences like duration and location to deeper inquiries about the personal or professional growth they hope to achieve.
- Interviews: Engaging in one-on-one conversations with potential or past attendees to gather detailed insights. This could involve asking about their past retreat experiences, what they found valuable, and what they felt was missing.
- Social Media Analysis: Monitoring discussions, comments, and shares across platforms to gauge interests and common themes among your target audience. This can also include analyzing hashtags related to your niche or conducting polls on platforms like Instagram or Facebook.

Fine-tuning Retreat Themes, Content, and Activities
With a wealth of data at your disposal, the next step is to

translate these insights into concrete elements of your retreat. This involves a careful process of selection and adaptation to ensure every aspect of your retreat, from the themes and content to the activities and overall flow, mirrors the needs and desires of your attendees.

- Themes: If your audience expresses a strong interest in personal transformation, for example, you might choose a theme centered around self-discovery and renewal. This theme would then inform the selection of content, guest speakers, and activities that support this transformative journey.
- Content and Activities: Based on feedback indicating a preference for interactive and experiential learning, you might incorporate workshops that encourage hands-on practice, group discussions, and outdoor activities that promote learning through doing.

The objective is to create a retreat experience that feels tailor-made for your audience, addressing their specific challenges and facilitating the growth they seek. This thoughtful curation of themes, content, and activities ensures that your retreat stands out as a deeply relevant and impactful experience.

Flexibility and Openness to Pivoting Based on Evolving Audience Needs

A crucial aspect of aligning your retreat with audience needs is the recognition that these needs can evolve. Staying attuned to this evolution requires a commitment to flexibility and the willingness to pivot aspects of your retreat in response to new insights or changing trends. This adaptability ensures that your retreat remains relevant and resonant, even as the landscape of your audience's needs shifts.

- Feedback Loops: Establishing mechanisms for ongoing feedback, both during and after retreats, allows for continuous refinement. This could involve mid-retreat check-ins with participants to gauge satisfaction or post-retreat surveys that solicit suggestions for improvement.
- Market Trends: Keeping a finger on the pulse of broader trends in your niche or industry can also inform adjustments to your retreat offerings. For instance, a rising interest in digital detox experiences might prompt you to incorporate unplugged sessions or activities that encourage mindfulness and presence.

Adopting a mindset of flexibility and openness to change empowers you to fine-tune your retreat dynamically, ensuring it remains a compelling and enriching experience for your audience. This approach not only enhances the satisfaction of attendees but also contributes to the longevity and success of your retreat offerings.

By placing the needs and expectations of your audience at the heart of your retreat planning, you create a foundation for experiences that resonate deeply and leave lasting impressions. Through meticulous research, thoughtful adaptation, and a commitment to flexibility, you ensure that your retreats are not just events but transformative journeys that mirror the aspirations and fulfill the desires of those you seek to serve.

The Power of a Differentiated Retreat Offering

In a market filled with options for personal and professional development, standing out becomes not just an advantage but a necessity. The key to capturing the attention of your ideal participants lies in the art of differentiation. It's about offering something not just different but decidedly better or more intriguing than what's already out there. This part explores how to navigate the competitive landscape of retreats, carve out a unique niche, and innovate in ways that leave a lasting impression on your participants.

Analyzing the Competitive Landscape

To set the stage for differentiation, you first need a clear picture of the current market. This involves more than a cursory glance at competitors. It requires a deep dive into what others are offering, identifying trends, and pinpointing gaps that present opportunities for innovation. This process reveals a saturation of silent meditation retreats but a scarcity of retreats combining meditation with creative writing or artistic expression. Such insights are gold mines for differentiation, pointing you toward unexplored territories ripe for your unique touch.

- Market Trends: Keep an eye on emerging trends within your niche. If wellness retreats are leaning heavily towards physical activities, there might be room for a retreat that balances physical wellness with mental and emotional health discussions.

- Participant Feedback: Listen to what participants are saying about existing offerings. Are there recurring wishes for aspects not currently being addressed? This feedback can guide you in shaping a retreat that fills these gaps.

Creating Unique Selling Propositions (USPs)

Your retreat's USP is its heartbeat, the core reason someone chooses your retreat over another. Crafting this proposition involves weaving together the unique aspects of your retreat into a compelling narrative. Your retreat offers a blend of professional development workshops and adventure sports in a location known for its breathtaking landscapes. Or it's the only retreat in your niche facilitated by experts from diverse fields, offering a multidisciplinary approach to personal growth. Whatever your USP, it should be clear, compelling, and central to all your marketing efforts.

- Unique Experiences: Focus on creating experiences that participants can't find elsewhere. This could be anything from a unique location to a novel approach to the retreat theme.
- Expert Facilitators: Leverage the expertise and backgrounds of your facilitators as a differentiator. Highlighting their unique skills and experiences can add considerable appeal to your retreat.
- Participant-Centric Approach: Design your retreat with a strong focus on participant engagement and

personalized experiences. Tailoring aspects of the retreat to individual needs or interests can set your offering apart.

Encouraging Innovation in Retreat Formats, Themes, and Participant Engagement

Innovation is the lifeblood of differentiation. It's what transforms a standard retreat into an unforgettable experience. This innovation can take many forms, from the structure and format of the retreat to the themes explored and the methods used to engage participants.

- Hybrid Formats: Consider blending in-person and virtual elements to extend the reach and impact of your retreat. For instance, pre-retreat online workshops can prepare participants for the experience, while post-retreat virtual follow-ups can help cement the transformations achieved.
- Thematic Depth: Go beyond surface-level exploration of themes. If your retreat focuses on mindfulness, delve into lesser-explored areas such as mindfulness in decision-making or creativity. This deep thematic focus can attract participants looking for a more profound understanding.
- Interactive and Experiential Learning: Move beyond lectures and seminars. Incorporate activities that engage participants in hands-on learning, from outdoor adventures that challenge their limits to artistic workshops that explore their creativity. These

experiences not only enhance learning but also make your retreat memorable.

- Personalization: In a world where one-size-fits-all is the norm, offering personalized retreat experiences can significantly set you apart. This could mean allowing participants to choose their adventure within the retreat or offering customized coaching sessions that address individual goals and challenges.

Innovation also means staying adaptable and ready to evolve your retreat offerings based on participant feedback and emerging trends. It's about creating not just a retreat but an experience that resonates on a deeper level, fulfilling unmet needs and exceeding expectations.

Through a strategic approach to differentiation, focusing on unique selling propositions, and a commitment to innovation, you can create a retreat offering that not only stands out in a crowded market but also leaves a lasting impact on your participants. It's about offering something genuinely valuable, an experience that enriches lives and fosters growth, setting the stage for a retreat that participants will remember and recommend for years to come.

Vision-Driven Marketing: A New Approach

In a landscape saturated with messages vying for attention, standing out requires a marketing approach that's not only strategic but also deeply rooted in the unique vision of your retreat. This vision-driven marketing doesn't just aim to inform; it seeks to connect on an emotional level, drawing in those who share your values and aspirations. Here, we explore how to harness the essence of your retreat's vision, crafting marketing messages that don't just reach but resonate with your intended audience and guiding you through the selection of channels and the art of storytelling to create narratives that captivate and inspire.

Crafting Marketing Messages That Resonate

The first step in vision-driven marketing is distilling your retreat's vision into key messages that speak directly to the hearts of your target audience. This means going beyond listing features and benefits. It's about conveying the deeper transformation that attendees will experience. Begin by identifying the core themes of your retreat—the transformational journey you're offering—and then translate these into benefits that matter to your audience.

For instance, if your retreat is designed to help corporate leaders harness mindfulness for better decision-making, your messaging might highlight the journey from stress and overwhelm to clarity and empowered leadership. This approach not only outlines the tangible benefits (enhanced decision-making, reduced stress) but also paints a picture of the emotional and professional transformation that awaits.

Selecting Marketing Channels That Align

The choice of marketing channels plays a pivotal role in the effectiveness of your strategy. It's not just about being everywhere; it's about being where your audience is most receptive. Start by creating a profile of your ideal participant—consider their demographics, lifestyle, and where they spend their time, both online and offline.

- If your target audience comprises busy professionals, LinkedIn and targeted email campaigns might be the most effective channels.
- For a younger demographic or one that values visual inspiration, Instagram and Pinterest could be more suitable.
- Don't overlook the power of niche forums or communities, especially for retreats catering to specific interests or industries. These platforms offer a space where your message can reach an engaged and relevant audience.

The key is to match the channel to the preferences of your audience, ensuring your messages are seen and heard in environments where they're already looking for inspiration or solutions.

The Importance of Storytelling in Marketing

At its heart, effective marketing is storytelling. It's about weaving narratives that bring your retreat's vision to life, engaging potential attendees not just with what they'll do or learn but how they'll feel. Storytelling transforms your marketing from a series of announcements into a compelling invitation to a transformative experience.

- Use Real Stories: Incorporate testimonials and stories from past participants who have experienced the transformation your retreat promises. These real-life narratives add credibility and emotional depth, showing potential attendees the change that's possible.

- Create a Narrative Arc: Every story has a beginning, middle, and end. Structure your marketing narrative to take potential attendees on a journey—from recognizing a need or desire (the beginning) through the challenges they face (the middle) to the transformation your retreat offers (the end).
- Visual Storytelling: Leverage photos, videos, and other visual content to tell your story. Visuals can capture the essence of your retreat's setting, the joy and connection experienced by attendees, and the tangible outcomes of the retreat in a way that words alone cannot.

Storytelling not only makes your marketing more engaging but also aligns it closely with your retreat's vision, creating a seamless thread that runs from the initial interest to the decision to attend.

In vision-driven marketing, the goal is not merely to fill spots but to attract individuals who resonate with the essence of what you're offering. By crafting messages that reflect the transformative nature of your retreat, choosing channels that align with your audience's habits, and employing storytelling to bring the experience to life, you create a marketing approach that's not only effective but also authentic. This authenticity is what ultimately draws in those who are not just looking for any retreat but are seeking the unique experience and transformation that yours promises.

CHAPTER 2
Understanding Your Audience Like Never Before

Imagine walking into a room where every conversation seems tailored for you – the topics, the jokes, the insights all resonate as if you were the one who picked them. That's the magic of truly understanding someone, and it's the magic you aim to recreate with your retreats. But before you can tailor experiences that hit home, you need a deep dive into who your attendees are – not just on the surface, but what moves them at their core.

Demographics vs. Psychographics: Crafting Your Ideal Attendee Profile

Gathering the Basics: Demographics

Start with the building blocks: demographics. This includes age, gender, occupation, marital status, and perhaps income level. Collecting this data might seem straightforward – surveys, registration forms, and social media analytics. Yet, it's what you do with this information that counts. For instance, knowing that a significant portion of your audience falls within the 30-45 age range tells you they might be at a stage where career growth, family life balance, or even health considerations are top priorities. This insight can shape not just the content but the timing and location of your retreat to suit their life schedules better.

Beyond the Surface: Psychographics

While demographics sketch out the outline, psychographics fill in the colors. Here, we dig into values, attitudes, interests, and lifestyle. Imagine you're planning a wellness retreat. Demographics might tell you your audience is predominantly women in their thirties, but psychographics will reveal if they're outdoor adventurers or if they prefer the quiet introspection of journaling and meditation.

Gathering psychographic information can be creatively done through:

- Direct surveys that ask not just about preferences but about daily routines, sources of stress, and life goals.
- Social media engagement: See what content resonates with your followers. Do posts about mindfulness exercises get more interaction than those about high-intensity workouts?
- Existing customer data: If you've run retreats or related events before, look back at feedback. What did attendees rave about, and what did they wish was different?

Creating Detailed Attendee Personas

With a blend of demographic and psychographic data, you're ready to create attendee personas – essentially, detailed profiles of your ideal participants. These aren't just useful; they're crucial. They guide everything from marketing messages to selecting guest speakers and planning activities.

Consider creating personas like:

- Eco-Warrior Erika: At 34, Erika is all about sustainability. She cycles to work and supports local businesses, and her idea of a great weekend involves a beach clean-up or a workshop on reducing waste. An outdoor retreat with a focus on eco-friendly practices would be right up her alley.
- Corporate Chris: 42, Chris is climbing the corporate ladder but feels burnt out. He's looking for a retreat where he can unplug, learn stress management techniques, and maybe pick up a hobby that doesn't involve staring at a screen.

Creating these personas involves:

- Listing their demographic traits.
- Describing their daily life, challenges, and aspirations.
- Identifying what they seek in a retreat experience.

These personas become your touchstone for planning. Every decision, from the retreat theme to the food menu, gets filtered through the question: "Would this appeal to Eco-Warrior Erika or Corporate Chris?"

Visual Element: Attendee Persona Template

Imagine a visual template for creating your attendee personas, complete with sections for both demographic and psychographic information, plus prompts to help you think deeply about their preferences and life challenges. This could be a downloadable PDF, or an interactive online form designed to make the process of defining your ideal attendee both structured and inspiring.

Textual Element: Real-Life Success Stories

Include a section in your materials or website dedicated to stories from past retreats. In addition to testimonials, use detailed narratives that show a before and after – perhaps a Corporate Chris who rediscovered his passion for painting or an Eco-Warrior Erika who learned new sustainability practices to incorporate into her daily life. These stories not only provide social proof but also help potential attendees see themselves in the experiences of others.

Understanding your audience at this depth does more than inform your planning; it transforms your retreat from a generic getaway into a deeply personal journey of growth and discovery. It's about creating that room where every conversation and every activity feels like it was designed just for them. By mastering the art of profiling through demographics and psychographics and bringing those insights to life with attendee personas, you set the stage for retreats that resonate, inspire, and, most importantly, connect.

The Art of Listening: Utilizing Customer Feedback in Planning

Listening actively to what past and potential attendees share about their experiences and expectations can significantly elevate the relevance and appeal of your retreat. This segment sheds light on effective strategies for gathering input, dissecting it to identify valuable insights, and weaving this feedback into the fabric of your retreat planning process, ensuring that every detail resonates with your audience.

Collecting Valuable Feedback

Gathering feedback is an art, requiring a mix of methods to capture the diverse voices of your audience. Consider these approaches:

- Surveys: Digital or paper surveys can be a goldmine of information when structured correctly. Post-retreat surveys help you understand what worked and what didn't, while pre-retreat surveys can gauge expectations and personal goals. Keep questions clear and concise, and always include open-ended questions to capture nuanced opinions.
- Focus Groups: Assembling a small group of past or potential attendees for a discussion can uncover insights you might not have considered. The dynamic of group conversation often brings out more in-depth

feedback. Choose participants from various demographics to ensure a wide range of perspectives.

- One-on-One Interviews: Sometimes, the most profound insights come from personal conversations. Reaching out to attendees for a one-on-one chat can reveal detailed impressions and suggestions for improvement. These interviews can be conducted in person, over the phone, or via video calls.

Analyzing Feedback for Actionable Insights

Once you've collected feedback, the next step is to sift through it for patterns, preferences, and areas begging for enhancement. This analysis can be approached through:

- Quantitative Analysis: For numerical data from surveys, use statistical tools to identify trends. How many participants rated an aspect of the retreat highly? Are there correlations between certain demographics and their satisfaction levels?
- Qualitative Analysis: For textual feedback from open-ended questions, interviews, and focus groups, thematic analysis is key. Look for recurring themes or phrases that indicate strong feelings, whether positive or negative. Coding responses can help in organizing them into meaningful categories.

This thorough examination not only highlights what you're doing right but also pinpoints opportunities for refinement. For instance, if a significant number of responses suggest that the pacing of the retreat felt rushed, consider adjusting the schedule to allow more free time or deeper dives into certain activities.

Feedback at Every Stage of Planning

Incorporating feedback into your retreat planning is not a one-off task but a continuous loop that enriches every stage:

- Pre-Planning: Use initial feedback to shape the core concept of your next retreat. What themes, activities, or formats have past attendees loved? What have they felt was missing? If you've never hosted a retreat, poll people who've attended similarly niched retreats.
- During Planning: As you develop the details of your retreat, keep revisiting the feedback. It might influence your choice of location, the balance of structured activities versus free time, or even the dietary options you offer.
- Post-Retreat Reflection: After the retreat, gather feedback again and compare it with your pre-retreat insights. This not only shows how well you've addressed past concerns but also sets the groundwork for future improvements.

Remember, feedback is not just about catching flaws; it's a window into the hearts of your attendees. It shows you what moves them, what brings them joy, and what they're seeking in their journey with you. By tuning into these voices, you ensure your retreats remain dynamic, evolving entities that continually strike a chord with those who experience them.

Visual Element: Feedback Collection Toolkit

Picture a comprehensive toolkit designed to assist you in

gathering, analyzing, and implementing feedback. This could include:

- Templates for surveys with a mix of rating scales and open-ended questions.
- A guide for conducting effective focus groups, including sample questions and tips for fostering open discussion.
- An outline for one-on-one interviews that encourages honest, detailed responses.

Interactive Element: Feedback Analysis Workshop
Imagine an interactive workshop where you learn hands-on how to dissect feedback for actionable insights. Through exercises, you'd practice coding qualitative feedback, using software for analyzing survey data and brainstorming ways to apply your findings to your retreat planning.

Textual Element: Case Studies of Feedback-Driven Success
Incorporate real-life stories from retreat hosts who transformed their offerings based on attendee feedback. These narratives would detail the feedback received, how it was analyzed, and the specific changes made to the retreats, underscoring the positive outcomes of listening and adapting.

By weaving feedback into the DNA of your retreat planning, you not only elevate the attendee experience but also foster a sense of community and co-creation. It's a testament to the value you place on each voice, ensuring your retreats are not just events but collaborative journeys that resonate deeply with those who embark on them with you.

Tailoring Retreat Experiences to Audience Desires

Crafting retreats that resonate deeply with participants involves more than just understanding who they are; it requires translating that understanding into experiences that speak directly to their desires. The magic happens when every aspect of the retreat, from the workshops to the meals, feels as though it was designed with them in mind. This section delves into the nuances of customizing retreat experiences, ensuring each moment feels personal and impactful.

Personalization in Planning

At the heart of a memorable retreat is the ability to personalize the experience for attendees. This goes beyond addressing dietary restrictions or providing a range of activities. It's about creating moments that feel uniquely tailored to the group and to individual participants. Here are strategies to infuse personalization into your retreat planning:

- Choice and Flexibility: Offer a menu of workshop options or activities, allowing participants to select based on their interests. For instance, a morning session might offer a choice between a high-intensity workout, a guided meditation, or a creative writing workshop.

This approach ensures participants engage in activities that resonate with their personal goals and interests.

- Customized Accommodations: Whenever possible, tailor lodging options to meet the diverse needs of your attendees. Some may prefer the solitude of a single room, while others might thrive in a shared space, fostering connections with fellow participants. Providing these options acknowledges and respects individual preferences.
- Interactive Content: Develop workshops and sessions that adapt based on participant input. For example, a session on work-life balance could start with attendees sharing their current challenges, which the facilitator then addresses through the content of the workshop.

Successful Tailoring in Action

To highlight how tailored experiences can elevate a retreat, consider the following examples:

- A wellness retreat for busy professionals incorporated an "unplugged" policy, recognizing that its attendees were seeking a break from digital saturation. The retreat provided secure lockboxes for devices, with scheduled "digital check-ins" for those who needed to stay connected for emergencies. This thoughtful approach allowed participants to engage fully with the experience, leading to overwhelmingly positive feedback.
- Another retreat aimed at creative professionals offered personalized feedback sessions. Each attendee submitted a piece of their work before the retreat, and

dedicated time was set aside for one-on-one reviews with experts. This direct, personal engagement with their work was cited as a transformative experience for many participants.

Going Beyond Expectations

The final step in tailoring retreat experiences is anticipating and exceeding attendee expectations. This involves not just fulfilling their expressed desires but surprising them with thoughtful touches that demonstrate your deep understanding of their needs. Consider the following:

- Welcome Packs: Curate welcome packs that include items tailored to the retreat's theme and the participants' profiles. For example, a pack for a mindfulness retreat might consist of a personalized journal, a selection of herbal teas, and a schedule of sessions, each annotated with a note on how it could benefit the specific attendee.
- Unexpected Free Time: In a packed retreat schedule, unannounced free periods can be a delightful surprise, giving participants the chance to process what they've learned, explore the surroundings, or simply rest. Announcing a surprise afternoon off following a morning of intense sessions can be a deeply appreciated gesture.
- Personal Notes: Leaving handwritten notes for participants, either at the start or end of the retreat, can add a deeply personal touch. These could express

excitement for the journey ahead or gratitude for their participation and contributions.

In essence, tailoring the retreat experience to your audience involves a meticulous blend of planning, personalization, and thoughtful surprises. It's about creating an environment where participants feel seen, understood, and valued—not just as attendees but as individuals on their own unique paths. By weaving these elements into the fabric of your retreat, you ensure an experience that not only meets but exceeds the desires and expectations of those who join you, fostering deep connections and unforgettable memories.

Building Personas: A Tool for Targeted Retreat Design

Creating attendee personas is akin to painting a detailed portrait of your ideal retreat participant. This process involves more than just outlining demographic information; it's about breathing life into the data and crafting a vivid representation of individuals who are the heart and soul of your retreat audience. These personas serve as a beacon, guiding not just the thematic and logistical aspects of your retreat planning but also shaping how you communicate your vision to the world.

Crafting Detailed Personas with Depth

The step toward creating these detailed personas begins with a blend of demographic and psychographic data, weaving together the tangible with the intangible to form a clear picture of who your retreat is for. Imagine you're painting a portrait, but instead of colors, you're using data points and insights:

- Start with the basics: age, occupation, and location. These are your broad strokes, setting the foundation of your persona.
- Layer in interests, values, and lifestyle choices. This is where your portrait begins to take on depth and character. What books do they read? Are they seeking tranquility or adventure? How do they define success?
- Add aspirations and challenges. Here, you're adding the shadows and highlights that bring the persona to life. What do they hope to achieve? What obstacles stand in their way?

This process isn't about creating a one-size-fits-all participant but recognizing the diversity within your audience. You might end up with several personas, each reflecting different segments of your audience.

Utilizing Personas for Informed Decision-Making
With your personas defined, they become a tool for making informed decisions throughout the planning process. Each choice you make, from the retreat's theme to its schedule, is an opportunity to align with the needs and desires of your personas.

- Theme Selection: Let's say one of your personas, "Adventurous Alex," thrives on physical challenges and outdoor exploration. A theme centered around adventure and personal growth in nature would resonate deeply with Alex.

- Scheduling: Consider the lifestyle of your persona. If "Busy Beyonce" is balancing a demanding career with family responsibilities, a retreat that offers flexibility, with core activities on weekends, might be more accessible for her.
- Marketing Approach: Here, your personas guide not just the message but the medium. "Digital Don" might spend a lot of time on LinkedIn for professional development, making it an ideal platform to reach him with ads or posts about your retreat.

Remember, the goal is not to limit your audience but to ensure that your retreat speaks directly to those it's designed for.

The Cycle of Refinement

Your personas are not set in stone. As you gather new data and feedback, it's crucial to revisit and refine them. This iterative process ensures your retreats remain relevant and engaging for your audience.

- After each retreat, compare the expectations and experiences of your actual attendees with your personas. Were there discrepancies? What new insights can you integrate?
- Stay attuned to broader trends that might affect your audience's preferences and challenges. For instance, a sudden surge in remote working might introduce new

needs for "Corporate Chris," prompting adjustments to his persona.

- This ongoing refinement turns your personas into living, breathing guides that evolve alongside your retreats, ensuring they continue to resonate on a deeply personal level with your audience.

By embracing the practice of building and utilizing personas, you're committing to a retreat design process that is both intentional and empathetic. You're not just planning an event; you're crafting an experience that acknowledges and celebrates the individual journeys of those you aim to serve, ensuring each retreat is as unique and dynamic as the people it's created for.

From Interests to Obsessions: Tapping into Deep Desires

At the heart of every decision to attend a retreat lies a desire more profound than a mere interest or a fleeting wish. It's about what keeps individuals awake at night, dreaming of change or growth. This section explores how tapping into these profound yearnings can transform a good retreat into an unforgettable, life-altering experience.

Unveiling the Psychological Drivers
Understanding why people are drawn to retreats involves more than just surface-level desires; it requires peeling back layers to reveal the core motivations. People are often propelled by a need for transformation, healing, escape, or connection. These motivations stem from a deep-seated

desire to fill a gap in their lives, whether it's personal growth, professional advancement, spiritual awakening, or social bonding.

- Transformation: Many seek a retreat experience as a catalyst for significant change, whether in habits, mindset, or life direction.
- Healing: Others might be looking to heal from past traumas, seeking a safe space to process and recover.
- Escape: The allure of stepping away from the daily grind to find peace or adventure drives numerous individuals to retreats.
- Connection: The desire for deeper connections—with oneself, with others, or with nature—is a powerful motivator.

Recognizing these underlying desires allows for the creation of retreat experiences that resonate on a profound level with attendees.

Crafting Content That Connects

Once you've identified the deep desires driving your audience, the next step is to design retreat content that speaks directly to these aspirations. This involves:

- Tailored Workshops and Sessions: Design sessions that address specific desires. For instance, workshops on mindfulness and self-care for those seeking healing or leadership and innovation for individuals aiming for professional growth.

- Engaging Activities: Choose activities that complement the sessions while also providing a practical application or a physical manifestation of the themes being explored. A retreat focused on connection might include team-building exercises or group hikes.
- Inspirational Speakers: Inviting speakers who have navigated similar paths of transformation or overcome comparable challenges can offer inspiration and practical advice, making the retreat's impact even more profound.

Case Studies: Connecting on a Deep Emotional Level
Several retreats have masterfully tapped into the deep desires of their attendees, creating memorable experiences that foster lasting changes:

- A retreat aimed at corporate executives incorporated silence and nature immersion into its agenda, recognizing the deep-seated need for escape and rejuvenation among its attendees. Post-retreat feedback highlighted a renewed sense of purpose and significantly reduced stress levels among participants.
- Another retreat, designed for individuals recovering from loss, centered around art therapy and storytelling. By providing a safe environment for expression and shared experiences, attendees reported feeling a sense of communal healing and personal closure.

These examples underscore the power of aligning retreat content with the core desires of attendees, offering them not just an escape but a transformative journey.

Understanding the psychology behind why people are drawn to retreats and crafting experiences that speak to their deeper desires requires empathy, insight, and creativity. It's about recognizing that at the heart of every attendee is a quest for something more—be it healing, growth, escape, or connection—and designing your retreat to be the bridge that helps them cross over to their desired destination. This approach not only elevates the retreat experience from good to transformative but also ensures that the impact of the journey continues to resonate long after the attendees have returned to their daily lives.

As we wrap up this exploration of how to tap into the deeper desires and motivations of your audience, we are reminded of the immense potential that lies in understanding and addressing these core needs. By creating retreats that not only meet but exceed expectations, you offer your attendees not just a temporary escape but a steppingstone toward lasting transformation. This endeavor, while challenging, is gratifying, as it allows you to play a pivotal role in the personal and collective journeys of those you seek to serve.

Moving forward, the principles and insights shared in this chapter lay the groundwork for the next steps in your journey—designing retreats that not only captivate and inspire but also leave a lasting imprint on the hearts and minds of all who participate.

CHAPTER 3
Crafting Sessions for Unforgettable Impact

Envision walking into a room where the energy is palpable, where every detail seems thoughtfully curated to spark curiosity, foster connections, and encourage deep reflection. This is the power of well-structured sessions within a retreat. They are not just time blocks filled with activities, but pivotal moments designed to engage, challenge, and transform.

Engaging Every Participant: The Key to Dynamic Sessions

The secret sauce to creating sessions that leave a lasting impact lies in understanding and catering to the diverse ways people learn and interact. Just like a chef adjusts a recipe to suit various taste preferences, tailoring your sessions to fit different learning styles ensures everyone gets the most out of the experience. Here's how:

- Mix It Up: Combine interactive, experiential, and reflective activities. This could mean starting with a group discussion to break the ice, followed by a hands-on workshop, and ending with a guided reflection.
- Know Your Audience: Ahead of the retreat, gather information about your participants. What's their background? Why are they attending? Use this to select activities that resonate.
- Visuals and Hands-on Learning: Incorporate visuals whenever possible and give participants something tangible to work with. This could be as simple as using flipcharts for brainstorming or providing materials for a creative project.

Pacing: The Rhythm of Engagement

Just like a day has its cycles of morning vigor and evening calm, your retreat sessions need a rhythm that balances high-energy activities with periods for relaxation and digestion of new insights. Paying attention to pacing ensures participants remain engaged without feeling overwhelmed.

- Morning Momentum: Use the natural energy of mornings for more demanding or interactive sessions. People are generally more alert and open to engaging with others.
- Afternoon Adjustments: Recognize that post-lunch, there might be a dip in energy. This is an excellent time for more reflective or individual activities.

- Evening Ease: As the day winds down, consider lighter, more social activities. Story sharing around a fire can be a perfect end to the day.

Breakout Sessions: Fostering Connections and Deep Learning

Breakout sessions, workshops, and group discussions offer powerful platforms for participants to dive deeper into subjects, share personal experiences, and learn from each other.

- Small Groups, Big Insights: Breaking into smaller groups allows for more intimate conversations and ensures everyone has a chance to speak and be heard. For workshops, consider grouping participants by interest or goal for more targeted learning.
- Facilitator's Role: In group discussions, facilitators can spark conversation with thought-provoking questions, guide the discussion to stay on track, and help draw out quieter participants.
- Share and Reflect: After breakout sessions, regrouping and sharing insights with the larger group can magnify the learning experience, allowing everyone to benefit from each group's discoveries.

Visual Element: Interactive Workshop Layout

Visualize an infographic that lays out the optimal setup for an interactive workshop. This visual guide shows how to arrange seating (circle, U-shape, or small clusters), where to place materials for easy access, and tips for creating a welcoming space that encourages participation.

Interactive Element: Participant-Led Sessions
Encourage participants to lead mini sessions on topics they're passionate about. This could be anything from a hobby to a professional expertise area. Provide a sign-up sheet before the retreat and allocate time slots for these sessions. It's a fantastic way for participants to take active roles and for everyone to learn something unexpected.

Textual Element: Reflective Journaling Prompts
Offer a list of journaling prompts that encourage participants to reflect on their experiences during the retreat. These can be general, such as, "What surprised you today and why?" or specific to a session, such as, "After today's workshop on mindfulness, what's one practice you want to incorporate into your daily routine, and how will you do it?"

By considering these elements - engaging various learning styles, maintaining a dynamic pace, and leveraging the power of breakout sessions - you set the stage for sessions that are not only memorable but genuinely impactful. These are the moments that challenge participants, spark new ideas, and foster deep connections, leaving a lasting imprint long after the retreat ends.

Integrating Personal Development into Your Business Retreat

In the sphere of business retreats, weaving in personal development activities isn't just an added bonus—it's a transformative strategy that propels professional growth in directions one might not anticipate. The seamless blend of personal prowess with business acumen offers a dual-edged sword of benefits: sharpening the mind for strategic thinking while fostering a resilience that sustains through challenges.

Enhancing Professional Capacities with Mindfulness and Meditation

Mindfulness and meditation, often relegated to the realm of personal well-being, hold untapped potential for professional enhancement. The calm and clarity achieved through regular mindfulness practice are invaluable in high-stakes business environments, where decisions must be both swift and sound. Meditation sessions tailored to focus on professional scenarios can help participants:

- Cultivate a sense of calm amidst chaos, enabling more precise decision-making.
- Enhance creativity, opening new pathways for innovation.
- Build resilience, equipping individuals to navigate setbacks with grace.

Incorporating these practices into your business retreat can be as straightforward as starting each day with a guided meditation focused on intentions for professional growth or integrating mindfulness exercises before brainstorming sessions to clear the mental clutter and foster innovative thinking.

Journaling for Insight and Breakthroughs

Journaling, a powerful tool for introspection, can also serve as a conduit for professional insights and breakthroughs. By encouraging participants to reflect on their career aspirations, challenges, and achievements, journaling can uncover underlying patterns and motivations that influence professional paths. Consider incorporating journaling sessions that prompt participants to explore:

- Moments of significant professional growth and the factors that contributed to them.
- Challenges faced in their career journey and the learnings derived from overcoming them.
- Future aspirations and the steps needed to achieve them.

These reflections not only offer personal clarity but can also spark discussions on common professional hurdles and strategies to overcome them, enriching the retreat experience with shared wisdom and collective problem-solving.

Guided Visualization for Achieving Professional Goals

Guided visualization exercises can be a potent tool in the pursuit of professional goals. By leading participants through a vivid imagining of their future successes, you help them establish a mental blueprint of their desired outcomes. This practice not only enhances motivation but also clarifies the steps needed to achieve these outcomes. Tailor these sessions to:

- Visualize achieving a long-term professional goal and the steps taken to get there.
- Overcome a current professional challenge, imagining different strategies and their outcomes.
- Foster a positive professional identity, visualizing oneself embodying the qualities of a successful leader or innovator.

These visualizations, grounded in the context of personal development, offer a unique perspective on professional growth, making the intangible tangible and the distant future achievable.

Weaving Personal Development into Every Aspect

The key to successfully integrating personal development into a business retreat lies in its seamless incorporation into every aspect of the agenda. This doesn't detract from the business focus but enriches it, ensuring personal growth and professional development go hand in hand. Strategies to achieve this integration include:

- Setting aside dedicated time for personal development activities, ensuring they are seen as integral rather than optional.
- Linking personal development exercises directly to business objectives. For instance, a session on mindfulness can be tied to enhancing focus for strategic planning.

- Encouraging participants to share personal insights in group discussions, fostering a culture of openness and mutual growth.

Visual Element: Personal Development Activity Guide

Create a visually engaging guide that outlines various personal development activities tailored for business professionals. This guide could include:

- A step-by-step breakdown of daily mindfulness exercises.
- Prompts for reflective journaling with a professional twist.
- Templates for guided visualization exercises focusing on career achievements.

Interactive Element: Personal Growth Plan Workshop

Facilitate an interactive workshop where participants craft their personal growth plans, aligning personal development goals with professional aspirations. This workshop could involve:

- Exercises to identify critical areas of personal and professional growth.
- Discussion groups to share insights and receive feedback.
- A template for creating a personalized growth plan, incorporating milestones and strategies for achievement.

Textual Element: Success Stories of Personal Development in Business
Compile a collection of success stories highlighting individuals who have leveraged personal development practices to achieve significant professional growth. These narratives should illustrate:

- The personal development techniques utilized.
- The impact of these practices on professional performance and achievement.
- Practical tips for integrating personal development into a busy professional life.

By embracing the power of personal development within the context of a business retreat, you not only equip participants with the tools for professional success but also foster a holistic approach to growth that nurtures both the individual and their career. This dual focus ensures that participants leave not just with enhanced business acumen but with a renewed sense of personal purpose and resilience, ready to navigate the complexities of the business world with confidence and clarity.

The Role of Mindfulness in Business Success

Mindfulness, once a practice confined to the realms of personal wellness, has found its rightful place in the business world. For professionals striving to navigate the complexities of modern business landscapes, mindfulness offers a toolkit not just for survival but for thriving. Its application reaches far beyond simple stress reduction, touching on critical aspects of business success such as decision-making, clarity, and emotional regulation.

Here, we explore the underlying science that makes mindfulness an invaluable asset for any business professional, practical methods for its integration into daily routines, and real-life success stories that underscore its transformative power.

Mindfulness, in its essence, is the practice of being fully present and engaged in the moment, aware but not overwhelmed by what's going on around us. For business professionals, this can translate into a heightened ability to focus, improved decision-making skills, and a more balanced approach to emotional responses. Research has shown that regular mindfulness practice can lead to changes in the brain associated with better attention, higher cognitive flexibility, and improved emotional regulation. These changes not only enhance personal well-being but also sharpen professional performance.

To weave mindfulness into the fabric of a business retreat, consider the following practical guidance:

- Start with the Basics: Introduce mindfulness with simple, accessible exercises. For many, the concept might be new, and starting with straightforward practices can demystify mindfulness and encourage participation. A five-minute breathing exercise at the beginning of sessions can set a focused tone for the day.

- Incorporate Mindful Moments: Schedule brief, guided mindfulness exercises throughout the retreat. These can serve as mental resets, allowing participants to digest information, regain focus, and approach tasks with renewed clarity.
- Mindful Listening and Speaking: Dedicate a session to the practice of mindful communication. This involves exercises in listening with full attention and speaking with intention. It's a skill that enhances collaboration and reduces misunderstandings in professional settings.

Mindfulness can be seamlessly integrated into the business agenda without feeling forced or out of place. For instance, a session on strategic planning might include a brief mindfulness exercise to clear mental clutter, allowing for sharper focus and more innovative thinking. Similarly, team-building activities can incorporate elements of mindful observation, encouraging participants to notice and appreciate the strengths and contributions of their colleagues.

Real-life case studies offer compelling evidence of the benefits mindfulness brings to the business realm:

- A tech startup introduced daily mindfulness sessions for its employees as a response to increasing stress levels and burnout. Over six months, the company reported a noticeable improvement in employee satisfaction, a decrease in absenteeism, and an uptick in productivity. Employees cited better focus and reduced anxiety as key benefits.

- A marketing firm integrated mindfulness into its weekly meetings, dedicating the first 10 minutes to a guided mindfulness exercise focused on gratitude. This practice led to meetings that were not only more efficient but also characterized by a positive, collaborative atmosphere. The firm attributed a significant part of its year-on-year growth to the improved team dynamics fostered by these mindfulness practices.

Practical examples of mindfulness application underscore its adaptability and relevance across different business contexts. From enhancing personal well-being to fostering a positive corporate culture, the benefits of mindfulness in the business world are multifaceted and profound.

Incorporating mindfulness into a business retreat not only equips participants with valuable tools for personal and professional development but also demonstrates a commitment to holistic success. It acknowledges that the well-being of individuals is inextricably linked to the health of the organization and that cultivating mindfulness is not just a personal choice but a strategic business move. Through guided exercises, mindful communication practices, and integrative techniques, participants can return to their professional lives armed not just with new business strategies but with a renewed mindset geared towards clarity, resilience, and purposeful action.

In essence, mindfulness offers a pathway to enhanced business outcomes through its focus on the present moment, fostering a work environment where clarity, decision-making, and emotional intelligence become the pillars of success. Its integration into the retreat schedule not only enriches the experience but also sets a foundation for practices that participants can carry into their daily professional lives. As mindfulness becomes woven into the fabric of business operations, its impact extends beyond individual achievements to shape a corporate culture that values focus, empathy, and strategic clarity.

Balancing Structure with Spontaneity

In crafting retreats that leave a mark on the hearts and minds of participants, a dynamic interplay between structure and the unexpected plays a crucial role. It's in those unplanned moments, where the agenda meets the authentic human experience, that true magic often unfolds. This section delves into how a well-thought-out plan can pave the way for spontaneity, fostering an environment ripe for growth, connection, and unforgettable memories.

Flexibility: The Gateway to Genuine Interactions

When we talk about flexibility in the context of a retreat, we're referring to more than just the ability to adapt to a change in weather or a last-minute venue switch. It's about crafting an agenda that breathes, offering spaces within the structure for organic interaction and the blossoming of unexpected insights. Imagine a day packed with back-to-back sessions, each meticulously timed down to the minute. Now contrast that with a schedule that includes open slots –

time intentionally left blank for whatever may arise. These available slots can become the breeding ground for impromptu discussions, self-organized breakout groups, or even a collective decision to shift the day's focus based on a shared interest or need that surfaces. This approach not only respects the natural flow of human curiosity and connection but also honors the unique direction that a group's collective energy might take.

- Open Time Slots: Integrate periods into your schedule that are intentionally left open. Inform participants in advance about these slots, framing them as opportunities for the group to shape the day based on emerging interests or needs.
- Participant Check-Ins: Regularly chat with attendees, both as a group and individually. Use these check-ins to gauge the group's energy and interests, which can guide the use of open time slots.
- Adaptive Facilitation: Encourage facilitators to remain attuned to the group's dynamics, ready to adjust their planned sessions in response to the group's energy and engagement levels.

Structuring for Spontaneity

While spontaneity, by its nature, can't be scripted, creating conditions that encourage unscripted moments requires thoughtful planning. This involves designing sessions that aren't just open-ended but actively invite participation and improvisation. Workshops that pose open-ended questions, activities that require collaborative problem-solving, or discussion circles where participants are encouraged to lead the conversation are all examples of structured yet flexible session formats. These formats serve as a canvas upon which participants can paint their insights, questions, and reflections, contributing to the retreat's evolving direction.

- Interactive Workshops: Plan workshops around tasks or projects that require group input and creativity, allowing the outcome to be shaped by the participants' collective efforts and ideas.
- Participant-Driven Discussions: Allocate time for discussions or forums where participants propose topics or questions, then lead the conversation, with facilitators stepping back into a supportive role.
- Improvisation Activities: Include activities that embrace improvisation, such as storytelling circles where participants build on each other's narratives, fostering a sense of play and spontaneity.

Empowering Voices: From Facilitators to Participants
A retreat thrives when every participant feels empowered to contribute, not just as attendees but as co-creators of the experience. This shift from passive participation to active engagement is key to unlocking spontaneous moments that enrich the retreat.

Facilitators play a vital role in this transition, setting the tone for a collaborative environment where everyone's input is valued and encouraged. This might involve facilitators stepping back at times to allow participants to lead or creating explicit opportunities for attendees to share their skills, knowledge, or personal stories.

- Skill Shares: Invite participants to lead mini-sessions or workshops based on their expertise or passions, turning the retreat into a mosaic of shared knowledge.
- Story Circles: Dedicate time for participants to share personal stories related to the retreat's theme, using a talking stick or another method to ensure everyone who wishes to share has the space to do so.
- Idea Incubator: Create a session where participants pitch ideas for group activities, projects, or discussions, then vote on which ideas to bring to life during the retreat.

By weaving flexibility into the fabric of your retreat's agenda, encouraging structured sessions that welcome spontaneity, and empowering every participant to shape the experience, you create a fertile ground for moments that resonate deeply and linger long after the retreat's end. These moments of unplanned insight, laughter, and connection often become the highlights of the retreat, remembered, and cherished as the points where something extraordinary happened. Through this careful balancing act between structure and the unknown, retreats transform into living, breathing experiences that reflect the collective spirit and individual journeys of those gathered, making each gathering unique and each memory irreplaceable.

Leveraging Nature for Deeper Insights

Nature, with its unscripted beauty and tranquil silence, offers a canvas on which participants can paint their

thoughts, dreams, and reflections. The integration of natural settings and elements into the retreat setting doesn't just add a backdrop; it actively contributes to the depth of learning and introspection experienced by each attendee.
The quiet rustle of leaves, the steadfast growth of towering trees, and the gentle flow of a nearby stream can all serve as powerful metaphors for personal and professional development.

These natural settings, inherently calming and inspiring, play a crucial role in reducing the noise of our daily lives, making space for clearer thought and enhanced creativity. Science backs this up, showing that time spent in nature significantly lowers stress levels while boosting the brain's ability to come up with new ideas and solve problems creatively.

To harness these benefits, consider incorporating activities that directly engage with the outdoor environment. Guided walks can serve dual purposes, offering a physical stretch while also encouraging participants to observe and reflect on the natural world's parallels to their personal journeys. Reflective journaling, when done beside a babbling brook or under the shade of an ancient oak, gains a new layer of depth as the serenity of nature encourages deeper, more honest reflections. Outdoor team-building exercises, such as raft building or orienteering, not only foster collaboration but also immerse participants in the beauty and challenges of the natural world, making the lessons learned more impactful and enduring.

However, the shift outdoors also necessitates careful planning to ensure everyone's comfort and safety. Here are some tips to keep in mind:

- Always check the weather forecast and have a backup plan. Nature is unpredictable, and flexibility is key.
- Ensure that all outdoor sites are accessible to all participants, taking into account any mobility issues.
- Be mindful of the environment. Leave no trace, respect wildlife, and choose activities that have a minimal impact on the natural setting.
- Provide essentials for outdoor comfort – sunscreen, insect repellent, water bottles, and suitable clothing recommendations.
- Finally, always brief participants on safety measures and ensure that everyone feels secure and informed about the day's activities.

By thoughtfully integrating nature into your retreat, you offer participants a unique opportunity to connect not only with themselves and each other but with the larger world around them. The lessons drawn from this connection – of growth, resilience, and interconnectedness – resonate deeply, often in ways that indoor sessions cannot replicate. Nature, in all its simplicity and complexity, becomes a silent teacher, imparting wisdom that participants carry with them long after the retreat concludes.

As we wrap up this exploration of leveraging nature for deeper insights, it's clear that the great outdoors is more than just a setting for retreat activities. It's a dynamic participant, offering lessons in growth, resilience, and the beauty of the moment. Through guided walks, reflective journaling, and team-building exercises, participants not only engage with the natural world but also uncover new layers of thought and emotion. Ensuring comfort and safety in these settings amplifies the experience, making it accessible and enjoyable for all. In this way, nature becomes a powerful ally in the journey toward personal and professional development, offering a quiet space for reflection away from the distractions of the modern world. As we move forward, we carry these insights with us, recognizing the profound impact that a simple connection with nature can have on our lives.

CHAPTER 4
Selecting the Perfect Locale: Where Transformation Meets Location

Wouldn't it be great finding a place that feels like it was waiting just for you and your group, a locale that whispers of potential and sings of renewal? The right setting does more than house your retreat; it cradles the aspirations of every participant, setting the stage for moments of clarity, growth, and meaningful connection. The quest for such a place is about more than just ticking boxes on a list of requirements. It's about finding a space that resonates with the spirit of your retreat, where every corner and every view aligns with the transformative experiences you plan to offer.

Criteria for Choosing Your Retreat Locale

Balance practical concerns with inspirational needs. When it comes to picking a spot for your retreat, the considerations are as vast as the locations themselves. The balance between practicality and inspiration is delicate. On one hand, the locale must meet logistical needs—size, layout, and affordability. On the other hand, it should be a wellspring of inspiration for all who set foot there. If this section feels overwhelming to you, remember that this is the Travel Agent's area of expertise. I highly encourage you to use one.

- Size and Layout: The venue must comfortably accommodate your group, providing spaces for both communal activities and personal solitude. Whether it's cozy corners for one-on-one discussions or spacious halls for group sessions, the layout can significantly impact the flow and feel of your retreat.
- Affordability: Keeping costs within budget without compromising on quality is a tightrope walk. It involves clear communication with venues about your needs and negotiating terms that benefit both parties. Here's where having a Travel Agent with connections and education can offer better pricing or exceed your original idea, creating massive value for your attendees.
- Alignment with Theme: A venue that echoes the theme of your retreat amplifies the experience. Planning a wellness retreat? Look for venues with natural tranquility. A creative writing retreat might thrive in a place steeped in cultural history or natural beauty.

Considering Participants' Travel Logistics

The journey to the retreat is part of the experience. A location that's too hard to reach may deter participants. Proximity to airports, train stations, or major highways, as well as the availability of shuttle services, can ease travel stress and start the retreat on a positive note.

- Accessibility: Choose a venue that strikes a balance between seclusion and accessibility. A remote island might offer unparalleled tranquility but consider the logistical challenges and additional travel costs for participants.
- Travel Support: Providing participants with a detailed travel guide or arranging group transportation from a central point can ease travel woes and foster a sense of community right from the start.

The Value of Site Visits

Nothing compares to the insights gained from experiencing a potential venue firsthand. Site visits—either in person or virtually—allow you to gauge the vibe of a place, ensuring it matches the vision of your retreat.

- In-Person Visits: Walking through the venue can reveal nuances photos cannot capture—the play of light throughout the day, the natural flow between spaces, and the comfort of the accommodations.
- Virtual Tours: Many venues now offer detailed virtual tours. While not a substitute for being there, they're invaluable for narrowing down options or when visits aren't feasible due to distance or restrictions.

Visual Element: Venue Comparison Chart

Create a chart that lists potential venues side by side, comparing key factors such as capacity, proximity to nature or urban centers, available amenities, and cost. This visual comparison aids in making an informed decision, ensuring the chosen locale ticks all the right boxes.

Interactive Element: Venue Selection Checklist
Develop a checklist covering all aspects of venue selection, from practical considerations like budget and size to more nuanced elements like ambiance and alignment with the retreat's theme. This tool ensures every detail is noticed in the hunt for the perfect venue.

Textual Element: Real-Life Venue Selection Stories
Include accounts from retreat organizers detailing their venue selection process. These stories can offer insights into overcoming challenges like budget constraints and logistical hurdles and finding a venue that truly resonates with the retreat's essence.

In the dance between practicality and aspiration, the right venue acts as more than just a backdrop. It becomes a silent facilitator, enhancing the retreat's mission and amplifying the transformative journey of every participant. The quest for the perfect locale is a step toward turning your vision into reality, creating a space where growth, renewal, and connection flourish.

Beyond the Venue: Creating an Atmosphere

Finding the right venue for your retreat is just one piece of the puzzle. True magic happens when you infuse the space with an atmosphere that breathes life into your vision, transforming mere rooms into sanctuaries of learning, reflection, and connection. This transformation doesn't happen by chance; it's carefully orchestrated through attention to lighting, decor, and layout, alongside the thoughtful integration of thematic elements and sensory experiences.

Setting the Stage with Lighting, Decor, and Layout

Lighting plays a pivotal role in shaping the mood of your retreat. Soft, warm lighting can make spaces feel welcoming and cozy, encouraging openness and vulnerability among participants. Natural light, where possible, uplifts spirits and energizes the soul, making it ideal for morning sessions. Consider using candles or fairy lights to create a serene ambiance during evening reflections or meditation sessions.

Decor, on the other hand, adds character and inspiration to the space. Choose pieces that reflect the theme and purpose of your retreat. For instance, a creativity-focused retreat might feature vibrant artwork and colorful textiles, sparking imagination and joy.

Conversely, a wellness retreat might lean towards minimalistic decor, with plants and natural elements promoting calm and clarity.

The layout of your space significantly impacts how participants interact with the environment and with each other. Arrange seating in circles or semi-circles to foster a sense of equality and community during group discussions. For workshops or individual reflections, create cozy nooks with comfortable seating, encouraging personal exploration and introspection.

Enriching the Experience with Thematic Elements

Every retreat tells a story, and thematic elements are the words with which this story is written. These elements should weave through every aspect of the retreat, from the activities planned to the very walls that surround your participants. If your retreat is centered on nature and sustainability, incorporate eco-friendly practices and materials throughout the venue. Use recycled paper for workshop materials, serve meals with locally sourced ingredients, and decorate with repurposed or sustainable items.

For a more adventurous theme, such as a retreat focused on personal breakthroughs and pushing boundaries, adorn your space with maps, travel memorabilia, and images of breathtaking landscapes. Provide journals adorned with quotes about exploration and discovery and use globes or compasses as decorative pieces to symbolize the journey each participant is on.

Crafting Memorable Sensory Experiences

The atmosphere of your retreat should be something participants can feel, smell, and hear, creating a multi-sensory experience that anchors them in the moment and deepens their engagement. Consider the following sensory touches:

- Scents: The power of scent in creating memory and mood cannot be overstated. Use essential oils or scented candles to infuse your space with aromas that align with your retreat's focus. Lavender and chamomile can soothe and relax, while citrus scents invigorate and awaken creativity.

- Sounds: Background music or nature sounds can significantly enhance the atmosphere. Choose tracks that complement the activities at hand—gentle, instrumental music for meditation or lively tunes to energize workshops. The sound of water, whether from a fountain in the room or a playlist of ocean waves, adds a calming element to the environment.

- Textures: Incorporate a variety of textures in your decor and furnishings. Soft throw pillows, smooth wooden surfaces, and crisp linen can all contribute to a rich tactile experience. Encourage participants to take off their shoes and feel the texture of the ground beneath their feet, whether it's cool tile, soft grass, or warm sand.

Visual Element: Atmosphere Mood Board

Create a mood board that visually represents the atmosphere you aim to create. Include images that capture the desired lighting, color schemes, and decor alongside samples of materials and textures. This mood board can serve as a guide in bringing your vision to life, ensuring every element contributes to a cohesive and immersive environment.

Interactive Element: Sensory Exploration Activity

Kick off your retreat with an activity that invites participants to engage with the environment through their senses. Provide them with a checklist of sensory experiences to discover within the space—identify a scent, feel a specific texture, and find a source of calming sound. This not only familiarizes them with the venue but also heightens their awareness and presence.

Textual Element: Thematic Decor Ideas List

Offer a comprehensive list of decor ideas tailored to various retreat themes. From bohemian chic for creativity retreats to serene whites and greens for wellness gatherings, this list provides inspiration and practical tips for transforming any space to reflect the heart and soul of your retreat.

In weaving together these elements—lighting that shapes mood, decor that tells a story, a layout that fosters connection, and sensory touches that ground and inspire—you craft more than just a setting for your retreat. You create an atmosphere that supports and amplifies the transformational work at the heart of your gathering, making every moment and every space a part of the journey. This purposeful curation of the environment plays a silent yet powerful role in the experiences and memories your participants will carry with them long after they've returned to their daily lives.

Navigating Budget and Accessibility Concerns

When it comes to orchestrating a retreat that's both

inspiring and inclusive, the dual elements of budget and accessibility play pivotal roles. The goal is to create an experience that's reachable to a wide audience without compromising the quality and transformative potential of the event. This delicate balance requires thoughtful planning and a bit of creativity.

Crafting Budget-Friendly Solutions

The quest for an affordable yet captivating venue need not be an uphill battle. With a strategic approach, you can uncover cost-saving opportunities that don't diminish the retreat's allure.

- Early Planning: Begin your search well in advance. This not only gives you a broader selection of venues but often allows for early booking discounts.
- Negotiation is Key: Engage in open discussions with venue owners about your budget constraints. Many are willing to offer package deals that bundle lodging, meals, and meeting spaces at a reduced rate, especially during their off-peak seasons.
- Consider Alternative Lodging: Hotels aren't the only option. Explore retreat centers, lodges, or Villa properties that can accommodate groups. These alternatives can provide a more intimate setting at a fraction of the cost. An experienced Travel Agent will have access to these types of lodging.
- Leverage Local Sponsorships: Reach out to local businesses that might benefit from exposure to your participants. They may be willing to sponsor meals,

provide materials, or fund a portion of the venue costs in exchange for marketing opportunities.

Ensuring Everyone Can Participate

An unforgettable retreat experience is one that's accessible to all who wish to join, regardless of physical ability or financial situation.

- Venue Accessibility: Make sure the venue complies with accessibility standards, providing ramps, elevators, and accommodations that ensure all participants can navigate the space comfortably. If you're considering an outdoor component, verify that paths and activity areas are accessible.
- Financial Accessibility: To widen the reach of your retreat, creative solutions can be employed to assist those who might not otherwise afford to attend.
- Sliding Scale Fees: Offer a range of payment options based on what participants can afford. This approach requires trust but can significantly broaden the diversity of your group.
- Scholarships: Set aside a portion of your budget to cover full or partial scholarships. This can be funded through a portion of full-paying participant fees or through donations.
- Crowdfunding: Launch a crowdfunding campaign prior to the retreat. This not only raises funds to subsidize costs but also builds a community around your retreat, engaging future participants and supporters.

Interactive Element: Budget Planning Workshop

Host a pre-retreat workshop (either live or via a web conference) focused on financial planning for attendees. This workshop could cover topics like saving for the retreat, finding travel deals, and other cost-saving tips. It's also an excellent opportunity to introduce the concept of the sliding scale and crowdfunding efforts, inviting participants to contribute or benefit, depending on their capability. If you partner with a Travel Agent, they may have partnerships with suppliers and vendors who offer payment plans and more.

Visual Element: Accessibility Checklist

Create an infographic or checklist that outlines key accessibility features to look for in a venue. This visual guide ensures that organizers don't overlook essential elements like doorway widths, bathroom accommodations, and accessible outdoor areas. It can also be a valuable resource to share with venues to clarify your needs.

Textual Element: Creative Funding Ideas

Include a section dedicated to innovative funding solutions for both organizers and participants. This could range from detailed guides on setting up a successful crowdfunding campaign to tips for securing local sponsorships and grants. Additionally, outline the steps for creating an effective sliding scale fee structure, ensuring it's fair and transparent.

Fostering an environment where every curious soul has the opportunity to attend your retreat requires a thoughtful blend of financial savvy, negotiation skills, and an unwavering commitment to inclusivity. By addressing budgetary constraints head-on and prioritizing accessibility in all its forms, you lay the groundwork for a retreat experience that's as enriching as it is reachable. Through early planning, open negotiation, exploring alternative lodging, and leveraging local sponsorships, the financial burden can be alleviated.

Simultaneously, by ensuring the physical accessibility of the venue and employing creative solutions like sliding scale fees, scholarships, and crowdfunding, you can open the doors of your retreat to a broader audience. This commitment to inclusivity not only enriches the retreat experience for all involved but also amplifies the transformative potential of the event, creating a vibrant tapestry of perspectives, backgrounds, and insights.

Local Partnerships: Enhancing the Retreat with Local Flavors

In the heart of every locale lies a treasure trove of experiences, flavors, and stories waiting to be discovered and shared. The decision to weave local elements into your retreat is not just about adding variety; it's about creating a richer, more authentic experience that resonates with both the spirit of the retreat and the essence of the destination. This section explores how fostering collaborations with local businesses and artisans can not only elevate the retreat experience but also contribute positively to the local community and economy.

Embracing Local Culture, Cuisine, and Craftsmanship

The integration of local culture and craftsmanship into your retreat serves multiple purposes. It grounds your event in the unique identity of its setting, offering participants a deeper connection to the place and its people. It could be as simple as incorporating local culinary specialties into your menu, giving attendees a taste of regional flavors, or as complex as including workshops led by local artisans, immersing participants in the area's cultural heritage. These elements not only enrich the retreat experience but also foster a sense of appreciation and respect for the local culture and traditions.

- Engaging with Local Experts: Invite local historians, artists, or naturalists to share their knowledge. A session with a local historian can provide fascinating insights into the area's background, adding layers of meaning to the retreat setting.
- Cultural Immersion Activities: Plan visits to local landmarks, markets, or communities. These excursions should be more than just sightseeing trips; they provide a hands-on opportunity to interact with and learn from the local populace.

Identifying and Approaching Potential Local Partners

The key to successful local partnerships lies in identifying businesses and individuals whose offerings align with the ethos of your retreat. It starts with research and outreach. Local tourism boards, online forums, and social media groups focused on the retreat's locale can be invaluable resources in this quest. When reaching out:

- Personalize Your Approach: Tailor your communication to reflect how the partnership could benefit both parties. Highlight the synergy between their offerings and your retreat's theme or objectives.
- Offer Clear Value: Be upfront about what you can offer in return, whether it's promotional exposure, direct business, or a long-term relationship.
- Respect and Adaptability: Show respect for their expertise and be open to suggestions on how best to integrate their offerings into your retreat.

Building Mutually Beneficial Partnerships

The most fruitful collaborations are those where both sides see clear benefits. As you forge these partnerships, consider how they can be structured to support the local economy while enhancing your retreat. A local farm can supply fresh ingredients for meals, offering participants a farm-to-table dining experience that also promotes sustainable agriculture. Or a partnership with a local craft shop could provide materials for workshops, allowing attendees to take home a handmade souvenir that carries memories of the retreat and supports local artisans.

- Transparent Agreements: Define the terms of your partnerships clearly. Whether it's financial arrangements, in-kind trades, or promotional exchanges, transparency ensures a smooth collaboration.

- Promotion of Local Partners: Utilize your platform to highlight the contributions of your local partners. This can be through social media shout-outs, mentions in your retreat materials, or a dedicated section on your website.
- Feedback and Follow-Up: After the retreat, share feedback with your partners. Positive testimonials can bolster their reputation, while constructive criticism can foster growth. This feedback loop strengthens the relationship for future collaborations.

Ensuring Respect for Local Traditions

While local partnerships offer a wealth of opportunities to enrich your retreat, they also carry the responsibility of honoring and respecting the local culture and traditions. This respect is fundamental to creating an experience that's authentic rather than appropriative. Engage with local cultural advisors to ensure that any cultural elements included in your retreat are represented accurately and sensitively. Moreover, consider how your retreat can contribute positively to the local community beyond the economic impact. Initiatives such as community service projects or donations to local causes can demonstrate your commitment to being a good steward of the place that's hosting your retreat.

In weaving the vibrant threads of local culture, cuisine, and craftsmanship into the fabric of your retreat, you offer participants a more immersive and meaningful experience. This approach not only deepens their connection to the locale and enriches their overall experience but also fosters a sense of global community and mutual respect. Through careful selection, respectful collaboration, and a commitment to mutual benefit, these local partnerships become more than just a feature of your retreat—they become a bridge, connecting hearts, minds, and cultures in a shared journey of discovery and growth.

Unconventional Venues for Unforgettable Experiences
In the quest to create retreats that resonate deeply and foster unparalleled growth, stepping outside the conventional can be a game-changer. Think of the stories that the walls of a centuries-old castle could tell or the creative sparks that might fly in an art gallery after hours. These unique settings do more than just host; they inspire, challenge, and elevate the retreat experience to new heights.

Unlocking the Potential of Unique Spaces
From the serene to the spectacular, non-traditional venues offer a backdrop that can transform a standard retreat into an extraordinary adventure. Picture the tranquility of a retreat held within an eco-friendly center powered by renewable energy and surrounded by lush greenery, fostering a deep connection with nature and a commitment to sustainability.

Or consider the allure of gathering in a historic site, where the echoes of the past bring a rich depth to discussions about legacy and personal growth.

- Historic Sites: Castles, ancient monasteries, or historic homes not only add a touch of grandeur but also ground participants in a sense of continuity and timelessness.
- Outdoor Camps: Immersed in nature, these spaces offer a canvas for exploration, both inward and outward, encouraging a break from digital ties and a reconnection with the natural world.
- Art Galleries and Studios: Surrounded by creativity, participants can find inspiration in every corner, igniting their own imaginative processes.
- Eco-Friendly Centers: These venues underscore a commitment to sustainability, offering a living example of how harmony with the environment can enhance well-being.

Navigating the Uncharted: Considerations and Solutions
While the appeal of such venues is undeniable, their unique nature often comes with its own set of challenges. Accessibility might be less straightforward than at a traditional hotel or conference center, requiring extra effort to ensure all participants can comfortably attend. Additionally, such spaces might need to be equipped with the standard amenities of more conventional venues, necessitating creative solutions for lodging, dining, and activity spaces.

- Accessibility Adjustments: For venues with limited accessibility, consider arranging specialized transportation or renting equipment to make the site more navigable for all attendees.

- Amenity Alternatives: Work closely with the venue to identify what can be provided on-site and what needs to be sourced externally. For example, if on-site dining isn't an option, local catering can offer a delicious solution while also supporting the local economy.
- Adapting Activities to the Space: Let the venue guide the choice of activities. An outdoor camp might be perfect for team-building exercises and nature walks, while a historic site could inspire sessions on legacy and personal history.

Inspiring Matches: Venue and Theme Harmony

The true magic happens when the choice of venue perfectly aligns with the retreat's theme, creating an environment where every element reinforces the retreat's objectives. This harmony between place and purpose not only enhances the overall impact but also leaves participants with a sense of immersion in the experience that goes beyond the ordinary.

- For a retreat focused on innovation and creativity, an art studio brimming with works in progress offers a tangible connection to the creative process, encouraging participants to embrace their own potential for innovation.
- A wellness retreat aimed at fostering peace and self-reflection finds its ideal home in an eco-friendly center,

where the principles of sustainable living mirror the retreat's focus on balance and harmony.

Selecting an unconventional venue requires a blend of vision, flexibility, and attention to detail. Yet, the rewards—a retreat that stands out for its uniqueness, depth, and transformative power—are well worth the effort. These venues do more than accommodate; they become a vital participant in the retreat experience, adding layers of meaning, beauty, and inspiration that enrich the journey for every attendee.

In crafting retreats that push boundaries and challenge expectations, the choice of an unconventional venue can be a powerful statement. It speaks to the adventurous spirit of the retreat, promising experiences that are not just outside the ordinary but deeply impactful. These spaces, with their unique stories and atmospheres, offer more than just a setting; they provide a source of inspiration, a catalyst for growth, and a backdrop for memories that last a lifetime. As we move forward, we carry with us the understanding that where we gather matters just as much as why we collect, reminding us that the path to transformation is as varied and vibrant as the venues we choose to explore.

CHAPTER 5
Crafting Your Retreat's Unique Value Proposition

Do you have something like a favorite coffee shop, where the barista knows your order and your name? There's comfort in the familiar, but there's also something exciting about a place that goes beyond the norm to create an experience that feels like it was made just for you. This same principle applies when crafting your retreat's unique value proposition (UVP). It's about pinpointing and articulating what makes your retreat not just another event on the calendar but a must-attend experience for your target audience.

Defining What Makes Your Retreat Irresistible

Spotlight the unique benefits and experiences.
Start by listing what participants will gain from attending

your retreat that they can't find elsewhere. Is it the unparalleled access to industry experts? The fusion of professional development with mindfulness practices in an idyllic setting may be possible. Or it's the personalized attention and tailored experiences that cater to individual growth. This step is crucial because it helps you move beyond generic features to highlight the unique benefits that make your retreat stand out.

Aligning with Your Audience's Needs and Desires
Next, take a close look at your target audience. What drives them? What are their pain points, and how does your retreat address these? For instance, if your audience consists of busy professionals looking for a break from the digital overload, your retreat could offer digital detox experiences in nature, combining relaxation with strategies for maintaining balance back in the real world. The key here is to make sure your UVP resonates with what your audience genuinely seeks, creating a magnetic pull that's hard to resist.

Brainstorming and Refining Your Retreat's Key Selling Points

- Grab a whiteboard or a large piece of paper and jot down all the features of your retreat. Next to each feature, please describe the benefits participants will derive from it. Seeing the direct line from feature to benefit can help crystallize your UVP.
- Ask for feedback. Reach out to past participants, trusted colleagues, or friends who fit your target demographic.

Their outside perspective can help you see which benefits stand out and which ones need more emphasis.

- Test and tweak your UVP. Use social media polls or email surveys to see how your audience reacts to different versions of your UVP. This direct feedback can be invaluable in refining your message to ensure it hits home.

Visual Element: UVP Flowchart

Create a flowchart that visually represents the journey from identifying the unique features of your retreat to articulating the benefits and refining them into a compelling UVP. This tool can be a reference for you and your team as you develop marketing materials and communicate with potential participants.

Interactive Element: UVP Workshop

Host a workshop (in-person or virtual) for retreat planners or entrepreneurs in your network. The focus is crafting a UVP that resonates. Break into small groups and have each team work on defining the UVP for their hypothetical retreat, using real-life insights and the brainstorming techniques mentioned above. This collaborative session fosters community and offers fresh perspectives on what makes a retreat irresistible.

Textual Element: Real-Life Examples of Effective UVPs

Include a section in your marketing materials or website that showcases real-life examples of retreats with standout UVPs. For each example, break down the components of the UVP—what features they highlighted, how they connected these to the needs of their target audience and the specific language that made their proposition compelling. This serves as inspiration and a practical guide for understanding how to construct a UVP that attracts attention and drives registration.

Defining what makes your retreat irresistible is an exercise in empathy and precision. It's about seeing through the eyes of your target audience, understanding their deepest needs and desires, and crafting a message that speaks directly to those aspirations. Like that favorite coffee shop, it's about creating a sense of belonging and anticipation, where participants know they'll find something tailored just for them—something they can't get anywhere else. With a clear and compelling UVP, your retreat won't just be an option; it will be the option for those seeking transformation, growth, and connection.

The Psychology of Effective Retreat Marketing

In marketing your retreat, tapping into the rich tapestry of human psychology offers a pathway to capture attention and kindle the desire for a deeper, more meaningful engagement with your offering. It's about moving beyond mere interest to creating a magnetic attraction that pulls at the core of your potential attendees' desires and aspirations.

Exploring Psychological Principles in Marketing
At the heart of effective retreat marketing lies an understanding of key psychological triggers that motivate a

person to act. When activated ethically and thoughtfully, these triggers can significantly elevate the appeal of your marketing efforts.

- Scarcity and Urgency: The scarcity principle leverages the human tendency to place higher value on things seen as less available. Urgency, closely related to scarcity, compels action by implying that delay could result in missing out. This could mean highlighting the limited number of spots available for your retreat or setting an early bird registration deadline.
- Social Proof: Humans naturally look to others when forming opinions or making decisions. Incorporating social proof into your marketing, such as testimonials from past participants or endorsements from respected figures within your niche, provides reassurance and validation to potential attendees.
- FOMO (Fear of Missing Out): FOMO taps into the worry that one might miss out on a rewarding experience others are having. Highlighting the exclusive experiences and transformations previous retreat participants have undergone can stoke this sense of FOMO, motivating others to join lest they miss out on a potentially life-changing opportunity.

Strategies for Emotional and Rational Engagement

Effective marketing messages strike a delicate balance between appealing to the emotions and engaging the rational mind. This duality ensures that your message resonates not just with the immediate desires of your audience but also addresses their deeper, more rational evaluations and concerns.

- Emotional Connection: Crafting messages that evoke an emotional response can create a powerful connection with your audience. This might involve using imagery and language that paints a vivid picture of the retreat experience, tapping into the feelings of tranquility, excitement, or discovery that your retreat promises.

- Inspiring Action: To move potential attendees from interest to action, incorporate clear, compelling calls to action that articulate the benefits of taking the next step. Whether it's the promise of finding clarity, enhancing creativity, or forging new connections, make sure your call to action resonates with the aspirations of your audience.

- Building Trust: Trust is the foundation for all effective marketing. Be transparent about what participants can expect, including detailed information about the itinerary, accommodations, and any prerequisites. Showcasing the qualifications and expertise of retreat leaders or facilitators can also bolster trust.

Balancing Emotional and Rational Appeals

Creating marketing materials that weave together emotional and rational appeals requires a nuanced understanding of your audience. It's about knowing when to tug at the heartstrings with promises of transformation and when to provide the reassuring details that answer the logical part of the brain's queries.

- Start by identifying the emotional drivers that might draw someone to your retreat—the desire for peace, a creative outlet, or the search for a more profound sense of purpose.
- Next, consider the rational considerations that could influence their decision—cost, location, time commitment, and potential outcomes.
- In your marketing materials, alternate between these emotional and rational appeals. For instance, after painting a picture of your retreat's serene, transformative experience, follow up with specifics about the schedule, activities, and tangible takeaways.

Visual Element: Emotion-Rationality Matrix

The Emotion-Rationality Matrix is an effective tool for ensuring your marketing materials balance emotional and rational appeals. This visual aid plots the emotional appeal of your messages against their logical appeal, helping you identify areas where one may outweigh the other and adjust accordingly.

Interactive Element: Emotional-Rational Appeals Quiz

An engaging way to involve your potential attendees in the marketing process is through an interactive quiz. This quiz can help them identify what they're most looking for in a retreat—emotional transformation or practical outcomes—and suggest tailored benefits of your retreat based on their answers.

Textual Element: Crafting Your Message Worksheet

To aid in the development of balanced marketing messages, provide a worksheet that walks through the process of identifying key emotional appeals and matching them with rational supports. This worksheet can guide crafting messages that resonate on both levels, ensuring a more compelling invitation to your retreat.

Storytelling Strategies for Authentic Promotion

In the heart of every individual, there lies a profound love for stories. This affinity towards narratives isn't just a means of entertainment; it's a powerful channel through which we connect, learn, and grow. For retreat organizers, tapping into the art of storytelling, opens up a realm of possibilities to showcase the transformative essence of their retreats, forging a bond with potential attendees that goes beyond mere interest to evoke a deep sense of longing and belonging.

Crafting Authentic Narratives

To capture the spirit of your retreat and the profound changes it can instigate in one's life, the stories you share must emanate authenticity. This authenticity acts as the soul of your narrative, making every word, every image, and every shared experience resonate with truth and relatability. Here's how to infuse your promotional efforts with genuine storytelling:

- Start With Your Why: Every retreat has a story of inception—a problem it seeks to solve or a dream it aims to fulfill. Share this narrative. Let people know why you created this retreat and how its journey began. This origin story adds depth to your retreat and helps potential attendees understand the passion and purpose driving it.

- Participant Transformations: There's no testimonial more potent than a transformation story. Encourage past participants to share their journeys—their hesitations, experiences during the retreat, and the changes they noticed in their lives afterward. These stories paint a vivid picture of what future attendees can expect, offering a glimpse into the potential growth awaiting them.

- Your Journey: If you're comfortable, sharing your transformation story related to the themes of the retreat can be incredibly impactful. It adds a layer of credibility and relatability, showing that you're not just the organizer but also someone who has walked a similar path.

Showcasing Success Through Various Media

The medium through which you choose to share your stories can significantly affect their impact. In today's digital age, you have a plethora of options at your disposal, each offering unique ways to connect with your audience:

- Blog Posts: Deep dive into the narratives you want to share through detailed blog posts. These can include interviews with past participants, behind-the-scenes looks at planning the retreat, or articles that tie the themes of your retreat to broader life lessons. Blogs offer a space for storytelling that's both informative and engaging, allowing readers to immerse themselves in the world you're creating.

- Videos: The power of visual storytelling cannot be overstated. Short videos that capture the essence of your retreat—the serene location, the joyous moments of connection, the peaceful sessions—accompanied by narratives from past participants, or you can evoke a strong emotional response. Videos are not just about showing; they're about letting viewers feel the atmosphere of the retreat and envision themselves being a part of it.
- Social Media Content: Platforms like Instagram and Facebook are perfect for bite-sized stories. Regular posts that feature snippets of participant stories, quotes that reflect the transformative journey, or even live Q&A sessions where you address questions and share more about what one can expect to keep your audience engaged and intrigued.

Interactive Element: Storytelling Prompt Journal

To assist in gathering the raw, authentic material needed for compelling storytelling, consider creating a "Storytelling Prompt Journal" for your retreat participants. This journal can include prompts asking about their feelings before, during, and after the retreat, specific moments that stood out to them, and changes they've noticed in themselves since participating. Not only does this help participants reflect deeply on their experiences, but it also provides you with rich, personal narratives that can be woven into your marketing efforts.

Guiding the Narrative Creation Process

While you have a treasure trove of stories, knowing how to shape these into compelling narratives is key. Here are some steps to guide you:

- Identify the Core Message: Each story should highlight a specific aspect of the retreat experience, whether it's the sense of community, the personal breakthroughs, or the serene environment. This focus ensures that your narratives are purposeful and impactful.

- Emphasize the Transformation: The most engaging stories are those of change. Structure your narratives to showcase the journey from initial skepticism or struggle to final realization and growth. This arc not only captivates but also mirrors the potential journey of future attendees.

- Keep It Relatable: Use language and scenarios that speak directly to the experiences and aspirations of your target audience. The more they can see themselves in the stories you share, the stronger the connection they'll feel to your retreat.

Through strategic storytelling, you not only illuminate the transformative power of your retreat but also invite potential attendees into a world brimming with possibility and change. In these narratives, the essence of your retreat comes alive, beckoning those yearning for growth, connection, and renewal. By crafting stories that echo with authenticity, showcasing them across various media, and guiding the narrative creation with a keen eye, you turn your promotional efforts into a compelling invitation, making your retreat an experience that cannot be missed.

From Features to Benefits: Selling Transformation

When planning a retreat, it's easy to get caught up in the details—the serene location, the expert-led workshops, and the gourmet meals prepared with local ingredients. Yet, when it comes time to share this experience with potential attendees, focusing solely on these features misses a crucial part of the narrative. The true essence of your retreat isn't just about what you offer; it's about the change participants will undergo as a result. This shift from features to benefits is where the magic of marketing lies.

Turning Features into Tangible and Intangible Benefits

The first step in this transformation is to look beyond the surface. Every feature of your retreat, from the morning yoga sessions to the fireside chats under the stars, serves a dual purpose. They're not just activities but steppingstones on a path to personal or professional growth. To communicate this effectively:

- List every feature of your retreat. Next to each, jot down the immediate benefit that comes to mind. For instance, a workshop on mindful leadership doesn't just offer insights into a new management style; it equips attendees with the tools to foster a more harmonious and productive workplace.
- Don't overlook the setting. A retreat nestled in a tranquil forest doesn't just provide a change of scenery.

It offers a chance to disconnect, leading to deeper introspection and creativity.

- Consider the meals. Cuisine crafted from local, organic produce isn't just about enjoying delicious food; it's an experience that revitalizes the body and instills a greater appreciation for sustainable living.

Communicating Outcomes Clearly

For potential attendees, understanding what they stand to gain from your retreat can make all the difference. This clarity helps them visualize the transformation awaiting them, and deciding to attend feels not just desirable but necessary.

- When describing the outcomes, be specific. If a session is designed to enhance communication skills, explain how this can lead to stronger professional and personal relationships.
- Use vivid language to paint a picture of the potential growth. Words have power, and the right ones can stir the imagination, allowing your audience to see themselves achieving their goals thanks to your retreat.
- Remember, the benefits of attending your retreat extend beyond the immediate experience. Highlight how the skills, insights, and connections forged during the retreat will continue to enrich participants' lives long after they've returned home.

Exercises for Identifying and Articulating Benefits

To ensure that your marketing speaks directly to the hearts and minds of your target audience, engaging them in a way that features alone cannot, consider these exercises:

- Benefit Brainstorming Session: Gather your team, or if you're planning solo, find a quiet space to reflect. For each feature of your retreat, challenge yourself to come up with at least three benefits. Push beyond the obvious to uncover the deeper value each element brings.
- Attendee Persona Mapping: Utilize the detailed attendee personas you've developed to tailor the benefits to specific needs and aspirations. What does each persona stand to gain from your retreat? This exercise ensures your messaging resonates on a personal level.
- Feedback Loop: Reach out to past participants for feedback on what they found most transformative about their experience. This real-world insight can help you hone in on the benefits that truly matter to your audience.

By focusing on the transformation that attendees will experience, your marketing does more than inform; it inspires. It shifts the narrative from what you're offering to what participants will become—a subtle but powerful distinction that can dramatically elevate the appeal of your retreat. In doing so, you invite your audience not just to a place but to a possibility—the possibility of growth, renewal, and profound change.

Leveraging Testimonials and Success Stories
The voices of those who have walked the paths of your retreats before, carry a weight of authenticity and trust that

any other marketing strategy can hardly match. Real stories from real people offer glimpses into the transformative potential of your retreat, acting as beacons for those still considering whether to take the step. Here's how to make the most of these powerful endorsements.

Gathering Impactful Testimonials

The process of collecting testimonials begins with reaching out. After your retreat, send a heartfelt note to participants, thanking them for their presence and inviting them to share their experiences. Make it easy for them by providing a simple form or guiding questions. Ask about their feelings before attending, the highlights during the retreat, and the changes they've noticed in themselves since returning home. Remember, the most compelling testimonials tell a story of transformation, so encourage detail and depth. If you've never hosted your own retreat, interview people who have had positive experiences attending retreats like yours.

Incorporating Testimonials Across Your Platforms

Once you have gathered these golden nuggets of praise and reflection, it's time to share them with the world. But don't just scatter them randomly. Be strategic in placing these testimonials where they'll have the most impact:

- Your Website: Create a dedicated section for testimonials on your retreat's homepage. Feature a mix of short quotes for quick reading and longer stories for those craving more detail.
- Social Media: Regularly share testimonials on your social media platforms. Pair them with photos or

videos from your retreats for a more dynamic presentation. Tagging the participants (with their permission) can also increase reach and engagement.

- Email Newsletters: Include a testimonial in each newsletter. This constant drip of real stories keeps the transformative power of your retreats top of mind for your subscribers.

Crafting Compelling Case Studies

Beyond individual testimonials, developing detailed case studies of past participants' journeys offers an in-depth look at the retreat experience and its outcomes. Select a few stories that particularly stand out and dive deeper:

- Interview the Participant: Have a conversation with them about their journey, focusing on specific challenges they faced, moments of insight or breakthrough during the retreat, and the tangible impacts on their life afterward.

- Use Before and After: Highlight the contrast between where the participant started and where they are now. This not only underscores the transformative aspect of the retreat but also makes the narrative more relatable to potential attendees who may see themselves in the 'before.'

- Include Visuals: Whenever possible, incorporate photos or videos of the participant during the retreat and in their life afterward. Visuals add a layer of authenticity and emotion to the story.

Maximizing the Impact of Testimonials and Success Stories

To ensure these testimonials and success stories resonate with potential attendees, keep these tips in mind:

- Authenticity is Key: Choose testimonials that feel genuine and heartfelt. People can sense when a story rings true, and authenticity breeds trust.
- Diversity Matters: Showcase a range of experiences to appeal to the broad spectrum of your audience. Different stories will speak to different people, so include a variety from various demographics, backgrounds, and outcomes.
- Update Regularly: As you host more retreats, continue to collect and share new stories. Fresh testimonials keep your content dynamic and show that your retreats consistently deliver transformative experiences.

In blending these strategies, testimonials and success stories become more than just marketing tools; they affirm the life-changing experiences your retreats offer. They bridge the gap between uncertainty and action, encouraging potential attendees to leap, assured by the voices of those who have journeyed before them.

As we wrap up this exploration into the power of testimonials and success stories, it's clear they are not merely endorsements but reflections of your retreats' profound impact on individuals' lives. They serve as tangible evidence of transformation, connecting deeply with those seeking similar changes. Moving forward, these narratives enrich your marketing efforts and reinforce your retreats' core mission: to facilitate meaningful, lasting growth in a supportive, communal setting.

CHAPTER 6
Digital Marketing Strategies for Maximum Reach

Picture walking into a room filled with chatter and laughter, where every conversation invites you in, and every story shared feels meant for your ears. This is the essence of building an engaging online presence for your retreat. It's about creating spaces that buzz with life, where every post, every page, and every email feels like a personal invitation into a world of transformation and connection. In today's digital age, your online presence is where these conversations begin, where the first connections are made, and where the journey towards your retreat starts for many.

Crafting a Home Base: Your Website

Think of your website as your digital headquarters. It's the central hub where people land when they want to dive deeper into what your retreat offers. Ensuring your website is inviting and informative is like ensuring your home is ready for guests—the welcome mat is out, the directions are clear, and the door is wide open.

- Clarity and Design: Keep the navigation intuitive. Just like you wouldn't want your guests wandering through a maze to find the living room, your website visitors shouldn't have to click through a labyrinth to find what they want. Use clear headings, a simple menu, and stand-out call-to-action buttons.
- Showcasing Your Retreat's Essence: Use high-quality images and videos that capture the spirit of your retreat. Visuals can convey the atmosphere much more effectively than words alone. Imagine a photo gallery that takes visitors from sunrise yoga sessions to laughter-filled communal dinners, making them feel like they're already there.
- Your Value Proposition Front and Center: Right on the homepage, make it clear what makes your retreat special. Whether it's the unparalleled expertise of your instructors, the unique blend of activities, or the breathtaking location, make sure it's the first thing visitors see.

Optimizing for Visibility: SEO

In the vast ocean of the internet, SEO is your beacon. It guides search engines toward your site, ensuring people looking for retreats like yours can easily find you.

- Keywords Are Key: Research and use keywords that your potential attendees might use when looking for retreats. Tools like Google Keyword Planner or SEMrush can offer insights into popular search terms.

- Content That Connects: Regularly update your blog with posts that incorporate these keywords and provide valuable information or insights. This could be tips for preparing for a retreat, stories from past retreats, or articles on the benefits of your activities.

- Local SEO: If your retreat has a fixed location, make sure you're listed on Google My Business and other local directories. This helps people in your area discover you when searching for nearby retreat opportunities.

Engaging Conversations: Social Media

Social media is where the chatter and laughter from our analogy come to life. Platforms like Instagram, Facebook, and LinkedIn offer a space to share the stories, moments, and insights that define your retreat, building a community even before the retreat begins.

- Consistency is Crucial: Regular posting keeps your retreat in the minds of your followers. Create a content calendar to plan your posts, mixing in promotional content, testimonials, behind-the-scenes looks, and valuable information related to the themes of your retreat.

- Engagement over Broadcasting: Social media is a two-way conversation. Respond to comments, ask questions, and create polls—anything encouraging interaction. These engagements build a sense of community and belonging among your followers.

- Authenticity Attracts: Share real moments from your retreats or planning process. Authenticity resonates with people. It makes your retreat feel accessible and your brand trustworthy.

From the welcoming digital spaces you create, to the conversations you foster and the stories you share, every element of your online presence draws people toward your retreat. It's about creating an environment where connections flourish, where interest is sparked, and where the journey toward transformation begins. With a well-designed website, strategic SEO, and an authentic social media presence, you lay down the digital pathways that lead right to the heart of your retreat, inviting everyone in for an experience they will remember.

Utilizing Social Media for Community Building
Social media stands out as a vibrant marketplace of ideas, a gathering spot where like-minded souls can find camaraderie, insight, and inspiration. Your retreat can truly flourish in this dynamic environment, transforming from a simple event into a thriving community. This section delves into methods for nurturing this community, ensuring that every post, comment, and share contributes to a space where potential attendees feel seen, heard, and valued.

Crafting Content That Connects
At the heart of any successful social media strategy is content that speaks directly to your audience's interests,

challenges, and aspirations. It's about striking a chord, creating moments of "That's exactly what I needed to hear" or "I've felt that way too." To achieve this:

- Share Stories That Resonate: People are drawn to narratives reflecting their experiences and dreams. Highlight stories from past retreat participants who've experienced significant growth or transformation. These narratives not only showcase the impact of your retreat but also create a sense of possibility for future attendees.
- Provide Value in Every Post: Whether it's a tip for cultivating mindfulness, a quick yoga flow, or insights into creative rejuvenation, each piece of content should offer something valuable. This approach enriches your followers' lives and positions your retreat as a source of continual growth and learning.
- Engage With Questions and Challenges: Spark conversations by posing thought-provoking questions or offering challenges that encourage reflection and action. This interactive content invites your audience to share their thoughts and experiences, fostering a deeper connection with your brand.

Leveraging Platform Strengths

With the plethora of social media platforms available, it's crucial to tailor your approach to suit the unique strengths and audiences of each. This means understanding where your potential attendees spend their time and how they engage with content on each platform.

- Instagram: With its visual focus, Instagram is ideal for sharing beautiful imagery from past retreats, quick video lessons, and stories that offer a behind-the-scenes look at your preparation process. Use hashtags strategically to reach a broader audience interested in similar themes.
- Facebook: The community-oriented nature of Facebook makes it perfect for creating event pages, facilitating discussions, and sharing longer-form content. Facebook Live sessions can also be a powerful tool for Q&A sessions, allowing for real-time engagement.
- LinkedIn: For retreats with a professional development angle, LinkedIn offers a platform to share articles, success stories, and insights that resonate with a career-focused audience. It's also an excellent place to network with potential collaborators and industry influencers.

Fostering Positive Interactions

The tone and atmosphere of your online community are as crucial as the content you share. It's important to cultivate a space where engagement is encouraged and celebrated. Here are some strategies for nurturing positive interactions:

- Prompt and Personal Responses: Make a point of responding to comments and messages promptly and personally. This attentiveness shows your audience that their thoughts and questions are valued, strengthening their connection to your retreat brand.

- Moderation With Care: While open discussions are vital, it's equally important to ensure that conversations remain respectful and constructive. Establish clear community guidelines and be prepared to step in when discussions veer off course, always with a focus on maintaining a supportive environment.
- Encourage Peer Support: Often, the most meaningful interactions happen between followers. Encourage this peer engagement by highlighting questions or experiences shared by your followers and inviting others to offer their insights or support.

In the bustling world of social media, your retreat's presence can be a beacon for those seeking transformation, community, and growth. Through carefully crafted content, strategic use of different platforms, and a commitment to fostering positive interactions, you can build an online community that reflects the spirit and values of your retreat. This digital gathering place becomes more than just a marketing tool; it's a vibrant community where potential attendees can start their journey towards transformation, supported by a network of like-minded individuals.

Email Marketing: Personalization Meets Promotion

In an era where our inboxes are gateways to the worlds we're interested in, email marketing emerges as a pivotal tool for connecting with those who've shown a spark of interest in the transformative experiences your retreat promises. This channel allows for a nuanced conversation, a space where the personal and promotional blend seamlessly, inviting potential and past retreat participants to continue their journey with you.

Cultivating and Segmenting Your Email List

A well-maintained email list is akin to a garden. It requires regular attention, nurturing, and an understanding that not all plants (or, in this case, subscribers) require the same care. The first step is gathering your audience and encouraging them to sign up through your website, social media channels, or at the end of an engaging blog post about personal growth and transformation. Once you have their interest, the real work begins:

- Segmentation: This is where personalization starts. By segmenting your list based on criteria like past retreat attendance, interests indicated during sign-up or engagement with previous emails; you can tailor your messaging to resonate more deeply with different groups.
- Permission-Based Growth: Ensure every subscriber has opted in to receive your emails. This complies with regulations and builds trust, as recipients know they're receiving emails they've expressed interest in.

Designing Email Campaigns That Captivate

With your segmented list in hand, crafting email campaigns that spark curiosity and maintain excitement becomes your focus. Each email is a touchpoint, an opportunity to strengthen relationships and keep your retreat at the forefront of their minds.

- Content That Engages: From insightful articles and personal stories of transformation to sneak peeks of upcoming retreats and exclusive offers for subscribers, your content should always add value. It's about giving, not just asking.
- Visual Appeal: A well-designed email can significantly increase engagement. Use images and videos that capture the essence of your retreats. A beautiful sunrise from your last retreat location or a video snippet of a peaceful meditation session can speak volumes.
- Clear Calls to Action (CTAs): Every email should have a purpose, whether it's to share new blog content, invite subscribers to a pre-retreat workshop, or encourage registrations for an upcoming retreat. Make your CTAs clear and compelling, guiding recipients on what to do next.

Best Practices for Email Frequency and Design
The rhythm of your email communication plays a subtle yet crucial role in maintaining interest without overwhelming your subscribers. Finding this balance ensures your messages are anticipated, not dreaded.

- Consistency Without Overload: Regular updates keep your retreat fresh in their minds, but how often is enough? This depends on your audience and the nature of your content. A monthly newsletter might be perfect for general updates, while more frequent emails could be justified in the lead-up to registration deadlines.

- Responsive Design: With more people reading emails on their mobile devices, ensuring your emails look great on screens of all sizes is non-negotiable. Use responsive design so your emails are easily readable on a desktop or a smartphone.
- Personalization Beyond the Subject Line: Using a recipient's name in the subject line is just the beginning. Tailor the content within your emails based on the segment they belong to. For past participants, reference their experience; for new subscribers, focus on introductory offers or information.

In the tapestry of digital marketing strategies at your disposal, email stands out for its direct line to those who've already signaled an interest in the transformative potential of your retreats. It's a unique space where personalization meets promotion, where every message can be crafted to speak directly to your audience's aspirations, needs, and memories. Through careful segmentation, captivating content, and mindful frequency, your email campaigns become a marketing tool and a bridge, connecting past, present, and future participants in the ongoing story of transformation your retreats offer.

Collaborations and Affiliates: Expanding Your Reach

In the vibrant tapestry of digital marketing, collaborations, and affiliations stand out as threads that can significantly extend the fabric of your audience. When you partner with influencers, alumni, or businesses that share a synergy with your retreat's ethos, you're not just amplifying your message; you're embedding it into communities that trust and value the opinions of these collaborators. This section navigates the terrain of forging these partnerships, ensuring they not only echo but also enhance the values and goals of your retreat.

Identifying and Approaching Potential Collaborators
The key to a successful partnership lies in alignment. Your retreat, after all, is a carefully curated experience that seeks to resonate on a profound level with its attendees. The influencers, alumni, and businesses you partner with should, therefore, mirror the principles and aspirations your retreat stands for.

- Research with Intent: Start by listing potential partners who have access to your target audience and embody the qualities your retreat promotes. This could range from wellness bloggers and travel vloggers to local artisans and eco-friendly brands.
- Personalized Outreach: Once you've identified potential partners, craft outreach messages that express genuine admiration for their work and clearly articulate the mutual benefits of a partnership. Highlight how collaborating could offer their audience value and align with their brand mission.
- Showcase Your Retreat's Impact: To make your proposal stand out, include testimonials or stories from past participants that highlight the transformative experience of your retreat. Visual content, like photos or video snippets, can also paint a vivid picture of what

potential collaborators can help their followers discover.

Structuring Mutually Beneficial Collaboration and Affiliate Agreements

For collaborations to thrive, they must be rooted in mutual benefit. This means going beyond surface-level exchanges to create agreements that provide tangible value to both parties.

- Transparent Communication: Be clear about what each side brings and gains from the partnership. Whether it's sharing revenue, offering free retreat spots, or cross-promoting content, all terms should be transparent from the outset.
- Flexibility and Creativity: Not all collaborators will have the same needs or be able to offer the same contributions. Be open to crafting unique agreements catering to each partner's strengths and limitations.
- Long-term Vision: Consider how these partnerships could evolve. Initial collaborations might start small, but with trust and success, they could grow into more significant, long-term relationships.

Leveraging Partnerships in Marketing Campaigns

Once you've established these partnerships, integrating them into your marketing campaigns can significantly boost your retreat's visibility and credibility.

- Co-created content: Work with collaborators to create content showcasing your brands' synergy. This could be a blog post co-written with an influencer, a workshop hosted by an alumnus, or a product bundle offered in collaboration with a local business.

- Social Media Spotlights: Use your social media platforms to highlight your partners and the unique perspectives or products they bring to your retreat. Tagging partners in posts increases reach and strengthens the sense of community around your retreat.

- Affiliate Programs: For influencers or alums promoting your retreat, setting up an affiliate program can incentivize them to share your retreat with their followers. Providing them with a unique booking code or link makes it easy to track the success of the partnership but also offers a clear way to share revenue generated from their referrals.

- In navigating the world of collaborations and affiliations, the aim is to create a network of support and promotion that benefits all involved. You can significantly widen your reach by choosing partners who align with your retreat's values, structuring agreements that offer mutual benefits, and creatively integrating these partnerships into your marketing efforts. This approach not only brings your retreat to the attention of a broader audience but also enriches the experience for your attendees, offering them insights, connections, and opportunities that extend beyond the retreat itself.

Measuring Success: Analytics for Retreat

Marketers

In digital marketing for retreats, the ability to capture and interpret data stands as a beacon guiding you toward more effective strategies. It's akin to navigating a vast sea; without a compass, it's easy to lose direction. Analytics provide that compass, offering insights into the performance of your marketing endeavors and illuminating the path to optimized future campaigns.

The Vital Role of Digital Marketing Metrics

At the core of any analytics strategy lies the selection of key performance indicators (KPIs) that align with your marketing objectives. These metrics act as signposts, marking progress towards your goals. Understanding website traffic sources for retreat marketers can reveal which marketing channels are most effective in drawing potential attendees. Engagement rates on social media posts and email open rates show how well your content resonates with your audience. Conversion rates, or the percentage of website visitors who sign up for more information or book a retreat, ultimately measure the effectiveness of your call-to-action prompts.

- Website Analytics: Platforms like Google Analytics provide a wealth of data on visitor behavior, from the pages they linger on to the journey they take through your site. This information can help refine your website's layout and content to serve potential attendees' needs better.

- Social Media Insights: Tools native to platforms like Facebook and Instagram offer detailed breakdowns of post engagement, audience demographics, and more. These insights can guide content creation and posting schedules.
- Email Marketing Software: Most email marketing platforms come with built-in analytics for tracking open rates, click-through rates, and conversions from email campaigns, allowing you to tailor your messages for maximum impact.

Setting Realistic Goals and Benchmarks

The journey toward successful retreat marketing is a marathon, not a sprint. Setting realistic, achievable goals provides a framework for measuring progress and keeps your marketing efforts focused. Start by establishing baseline metrics based on past performance, then set incremental goals for improvement. For example, if your current email campaign has a 20% open rate, aim to increase it to 25% within a certain timeframe. These benchmarks serve as milestones, motivating you and your team as you witness tangible signs of progress.

Utilizing Analytics to Inform Decision-Making

Analytics do more than measure success; they offer a roadmap for continuous improvement. By closely monitoring your chosen metrics, you can identify what's working and, perhaps more importantly, what isn't. This data-driven approach allows for informed decisions on where to allocate resources for maximum return on investment (ROI).

- Identify High-Performing Channels: If your retreat's Instagram account drives more engagement and conversions than other platforms, it might be wise to focus more energy and resources there.
- Content Optimization: Analytics can show you which types of content resonate most with your audience. This insight can shape your content strategy, ensuring you produce more of what your audience loves.
- A/B Testing: With analytics, you can conduct A/B tests on different marketing elements, from email subject lines to landing page designs. By comparing performance, you can continually refine your approach for better results.

In a landscape as dynamic as digital marketing, the power of analytics cannot be overstated. They provide clarity in a sea of data, guiding your strategies precisely and purposefully. By embracing these tools, you elevate your marketing efforts and ensure that solid data back every decision. This approach enhances the effectiveness of your campaigns and ensures that your retreats reach those who stand to benefit the most. As we move forward, remember that the journey of a thousand miles begins with a single step, and with analytics as your guide, each step takes you closer to your destination.

In wrapping up, it becomes clear that the art of measuring success in retreat marketing transcends mere numbers. It's about understanding the stories these numbers tell, the insights they reveal, and the decisions they inform. As we pivot towards our next chapter, we carry with us the knowledge that in analytics lies the power to not just dream about success but to plan for it, track it, and ultimately achieve it.

CHAPTER 7
Pricing Your Retreat for Success

Have you ever been at a bustling local market? Stalls stretch as far as the eye can see, each offering something unique: spices that promise to add zest to any dish, handwoven textiles in a riot of colors, and pottery that melds function with art. You're not just browsing; you're on a mission to find the perfect gifts for friends back home. As you navigate through the market, what catches your eye isn't just what's on offer but the stories behind those items, the craftsmanship, the way they fit into your budget, and how they match the preferences of your friends. This market scene is similar to pricing your retreat. It's about finding that sweet spot where your value aligns perfectly with your participants' willingness to invest, ensuring that everyone feels enriched by the exchange.

Understanding the Costs: From Venue to Value-Adds

The Foundation of a Sound Pricing Strategy

Before setting any prices, it is crucial to get a clear picture of what it costs to bring your retreat to life. This is about more than just the big-ticket items like the venue rental or instructor fees. It's also about those often-overlooked expenses that can sneak up on you. Think about the analogy of planning a dinner party. You might have the cost of the main dish in mind, but have you considered the appetizers, drinks, or even the gas it takes to pick up all the ingredients?

- Cataloging Costs: List every conceivable cost associated with your retreat. From the obvious ones like lodging and food to less apparent expenses such as insurance, marketing, and your time spent planning.
- Hidden Expenses: Don't forget to factor in those sneaky costs. Maybe the extra fees for using credit card payments or the cost of decorations to make the space feel welcoming.
- Contingency Budgets: Just as you might keep extra ingredients on hand in case of a cooking mishap, establish a contingency fund for unexpected expenses. Setting aside 10-15% of your overall budget is a rule of thumb. This safety net can help you navigate surprises without derailing your financial plan.

Strategies for Cost-Efficient Planning

With a comprehensive list, the next step is to make your budget work as hard as possible. Here are some strategies to stretch your dollars further without compromising the quality of your retreat:

- Leverage Relationships: Negotiate with vendors or venues where you have a good relationship. Sometimes, being a repeat customer or promising future business can secure a better deal.
- Bulk Buying: For items you'll need a lot of (like workshop materials), bulk buying can lead to significant savings.
- DIY Where Feasible: There's a unique charm in handmade or personally curated elements. Creating your welcome packs or decorations saves money and adds a personal touch that participants will appreciate.

Visual Element: Cost Breakdown Chart

A pie chart that visually breaks down the typical costs of hosting a retreat can be incredibly enlightening. Seeing how much goes into lodging, food, activities, and other categories at a glance, helps you understand where your money is going and where you might have room to adjust.

Interactive Element: Budget Planner Tool

A digital budget planner tool designed for retreat planning could be a game-changer. You can see how changes in one area affect the overall budget by inputting different costs. Including a section for hidden expenses and a contingency fund can help ensure you cover all your bases.

Planning a retreat is a lot like that journey through the market. You have a vision of what you want to create, a budget, and the challenge of finding just the right mix of elements to make it all come together. Understanding your costs is the first step in that process, laying the groundwork for a pricing strategy that ensures your retreat is memorable and financially viable.

Models of Pricing: Finding What Works for You

Deciding on a pricing model for your retreat is akin to selecting the right frame for a piece of art. The content—the transformative experience of the retreat—remains constant, but the frame—the pricing model—can significantly influence how your audience perceives and accesses this experience. Let's explore three primary pricing structures, flat-rate, tiered, and all-inclusive, to identify which best suits your retreat's unique canvas.

Flat-Rate Pricing: Simplicity Meets Transparency

Flat-rate pricing is straightforward: one price grants access to all aspects of the retreat. This model's simplicity and transparency makes it easy for potential participants to understand and decide without navigating a maze of options.

- Benefits: The precise, all-encompassing nature of flat-rate pricing eliminates confusion, making it appealing for retreats focusing on inclusivity and simplicity. It's a breeze to communicate and market, as you offer a comprehensive package.
- Drawbacks: This model's simplicity can also be its downfall. It leaves little room for flexibility or customization, which might deter attendees looking for

a more personalized retreat experience or those with varying budgetary constraints.

- Case Study: A mountain wellness retreat adopted flat-rate pricing, emphasizing the ease of decision-making for guests. Feedback highlighted appreciation for the straightforward approach, although some wished for optional add-ons to tailor their experience further.

Tiered Pricing: Flexibility for Diverse Needs

Tiered pricing introduces layers to the retreat experience, offering basic to premium packages with varying access levels and perks. This model caters to a broader audience by providing options that accommodate different budgets and preferences.

- Benefits: The greatest strength of tiered pricing lies in its adaptability. Attendees can choose a package that aligns with their interests and financial capacity, making the retreat accessible to a broader audience. It also opens additional revenue streams by offering upsells and add-ons.
- Drawbacks: The complexity of managing multiple packages can be a challenge. It requires clear communication to ensure attendees understand what each tier offers. Depending on their chosen tier, there's also the risk of creating a divided experience among participants.
- Case Study: An international yoga retreat implemented tiered pricing, offering varying accommodation levels and session access. The model attracted diverse

attendees, though feedback suggested a desire for more communal activities across tiers.

All-Inclusive Pricing: The Ultimate in Convenience

All-inclusive pricing combines the concept of simplicity from flat-rate models with the comprehensive nature of luxury offerings. This model ensures that once attendees pay, they need not worry about any additional costs, covering everything from accommodations and meals to workshops and excursions.

- Benefits: The all-inclusive model epitomizes hassle-free planning for participants. It promises a worry-free experience that focuses on personal growth and enjoyment, not on navigating extra costs. For retreat organizers, it simplifies budgeting and financial management.
- Drawbacks: The higher upfront cost can be a barrier for some potential attendees. Additionally, the all-inclusive nature might deter those who prefer choosing and paying for only the aspects of the retreat that interest them.
- Case Study: A creative writing retreat on a secluded island adopted an all-inclusive pricing model, covering workshops, private coaching sessions, and leisure activities. Attendees praised the model's ease and peace of mind, though some noted they would have appreciated a lower-cost option without certain extras.

Each pricing model offers a unique frame through which participants can view and experience your retreat. The choice between them isn't just about numbers; it's about aligning with your retreat's ethos and the expectations of your target audience. Consider the following when making your decision:

- Audience Demographics: Understanding the financial flexibility of your target participants can guide you toward a pricing model that matches their capabilities and expectations.
- Market Research: Investigate similar retreats and their pricing structures. What seems to be working for them? How do participants respond to different pricing models?
- Retreat Goals: Reflect on the primary goal of your retreat. Is it to provide an exclusive, high-end experience or to make personal growth accessible to as many people as possible?

Ultimately, selecting the suitable pricing model for your retreat requires a delicate balance between financial viability and the value you're offering to your participants. It's about creating a frame that complements and enhances the transformative experience at the heart of your retreat.

Communicating Value in Your Pricing Strategy

In the landscape of hosting retreats, where experiences are rich and transformative, setting a price tag can often feel like trying to quantify the unquantifiable. The magic of a retreat doesn't just lie in its serene settings or well-structured sessions; it's in the profound personal shifts that participants experience. So, how do you ensure that the price reflects this immense value? The key lies in effective communication.

Making the Unique Experiences Shine

Every retreat offers a unique blend of experiences, and these should be at the forefront of your pricing conversation. It's not just about the 'what'—the 'how' and the 'why' resonate with potential attendees.

- Spotlight on Facilitators: People are drawn to stories and expertise. Highlight the journey and credentials of your facilitators. A seasoned meditation teacher who's traveled the world or a creativity coach who's helped hundreds find their muse can significantly elevate the perceived value of your retreat.
- Exclusive Experiences: If your retreat offers something that participants can't find anywhere else—a particular blend of activities, access to sacred sites, or a unique cultural immersion—make sure this is front and center in your messaging. These are your value amplifiers.

Crafting Compelling Narratives

The art of storytelling can transform your retreat's value proposition from a simple transaction to an irresistible invitation. The narrative should weave a tapestry that showcases what attendees will experience and why it matters.

- The Transformation Arc: Use narratives that detail the journey of transformation attendees can expect. From the initial longing for change or growth to the breakthrough moments and the lasting impacts, stories that chart this arc can powerfully convey the value of your retreat.

- Testimonials and Success Stories: There's nothing quite like hearing about the transformative experiences of past attendees to spark interest. These stories are concrete examples of the value your retreat offers, making the investment seem worthwhile and essential.

Transparency Builds Trust

In any relationship, trust is foundational, which also holds true in the retreat attendee-organizer relationship. Regarding pricing, transparency isn't just a good practice; it's pivotal.

- Clear Breakdowns: Ensure your pricing page or brochure breaks down what the fee covers. From accommodations and meals to sessions and materials, knowing exactly what their investment entails helps attendees feel secure in their decisions.
- No Hidden Costs: Be upfront about any additional costs that might occur, such as travel to the retreat site, optional excursions, or special sessions. Surprises are lovely, but not when it comes to fees.
- Value Justification: Use your platforms to explain the pricing. This could be through a detailed FAQ on your website, a dedicated email explaining the value or even a video message where you share the heart and soul poured into creating the retreat. When attendees understand the care, expertise, and intention behind

the retreat, the price becomes a reflection of value, not just a number.

There lies inherent value in every aspect of your retreat—from the serene dawn yoga sessions that promise to rejuvenate the body and soul to the intimate workshops that spark profound insights. When communicated effectively, this value transforms your pricing from a hurdle to be overcome into a testament to the transformative experiences you offer. It assures potential attendees that their investment goes beyond the tangible; it invests in growth, healing, and unforgettable memories. Through highlighting the unique experiences, weaving compelling narratives, and maintaining transparency, you invite attendees into a space where the value is clear, compelling them to leap into an experience that promises so much more than can be quantified.

Early Bird and Tiered Pricing Techniques

In the dynamic world of retreat planning, crafting a pricing strategy that appeals to your target audience and enhances your financial sustainability is akin to finding the perfect rhythm in a melody. It's about striking the right notes that resonate with your audience's expectations and business goals. Among the most harmonious techniques in this symphony of pricing are early bird and tiered pricing. These strategies sing to the tune of incentivizing commitment and managing the flow of your retreat's registrations, creating a cadence that encourages early sign-ups and rewards those who act promptly.

The Mechanics of Early Bird Pricing

Imagine a scenario where the allure of saving on the cost of attending your retreat motivates potential participants to register sooner rather than later. This is the essence of early bird pricing. It's a simple yet effective tactic: offer a reduced rate for those who commit to your retreat within a specified early period. The beauty of this approach lies in its dual benefits. For your attendees, it's an opportunity to save on the cost of an experience they're already interested in. For you, it generates early registrations, providing a clearer picture of attendance numbers well in advance of your retreat.

- Creating Urgency: The key to maximizing the impact of early bird pricing is carefully crafting its deadline. A well-considered deadline creates a sense of urgency, compelling potential attendees to take action to avoid missing out on the savings.
- Setting the Right Discount: Determining the discount requires a delicate balance. It must be significant enough to motivate early registration but not so large that it undermines your retreat's perceived value or profitability.

Structuring Tiered Pricing to Reward Early Commitment

While early bird pricing is like a sprint, encouraging a quick start, tiered pricing is more of a marathon, offering sustained motivation over a more extended period. This model involves setting up different pricing levels that increase as your retreat date approaches. Each tier is priced slightly higher than the last, rewarding those who commit early and providing a gentle push for those still on the fence as the retreat nears.

- Incremental Increases: The success of tiered pricing hinges on the incremental nature of the price increases. Each new tier should reflect a slight but noticeable price rise, offering a clear incentive for early decision-making.
- Communicating Value at Every Tier: Each pricing tier must be accompanied by clear communication about the value provided. This ensures that even as prices increase, the focus remains on the rich experiences and transformations your retreat promises.

Effective Communication of Pricing Strategies

The melody of your pricing strategy reaches its crescendo in how you communicate these opportunities to your audience. Transparent, creative, and engaging communication ensures that your early bird and tiered pricing strategies harmonize with the expectations and desires of your potential attendees.

- Clear Visuals: Graphics and charts that visually depict the savings of early bird pricing or tiered pricing structure can be incredibly effective. They provide an immediate, understandable reference for potential attendees evaluating their options.

- Timely Reminders: Utilize your email list and social media channels to send gentle reminders as the end of an early bird period or the transition to a higher pricing tier approaches. These reminders can be framed to emphasize the benefits of acting now, such as highlighting what past participants have gained from the retreat experience.
- Engaging Content: Beyond mere announcements, create content that weaves the narrative of your retreat's transformative potential with the practicalities of your pricing strategy. Storytelling that connects the dots between early commitment and the anticipation of the retreat experience can motivate action in a natural and compelling way.

Ultimately, early bird and tiered pricing rhythms are not just about numbers. They play a critical role in the larger composition of your retreat's success, from financial viability to creating a community of eager and committed participants. Like any good melody, the right pricing strategy stays with you, setting the tone for an experience that promises to be both enriching and unforgettable.

Handling Discounts and Scholarships

In the realm of hosting retreats, crafting an experience that's both enriching and accessible is akin to painting on a vast canvas. It demands a careful blend of colors, techniques, and textures to create a masterpiece that speaks to all who gaze upon it. In this spirit, integrating discounts and scholarships into your pricing strategy is not merely about adjusting numbers; it's about weaving a richer tapestry of community, diversity, and inclusivity into the fabric of your retreat.

Strategic Use of Discounts

When applied with intention, discounts serve as a powerful tool to enhance attendance while safeguarding the retreat's financial health. Here are some strategies that strike this balance effectively:

- Group Discounts: Encourage attendees to bring friends or colleagues by offering reduced rates for group registrations. This fills your retreat more quickly and fosters a sense of community before the retreat even begins. I train Travel Agents on booking groups by having them ask this simple question, "Who else do you know who would want to join you?"
- Referral Incentives: Implement a referral program where past attendees receive a discount on future retreats for every new participant they refer. This leverages the trust and enthusiasm of your alums to attract new faces.
- Early Registration Rewards: Beyond the typical early bird pricing, consider additional perks for early registrants, such as exclusive sessions with facilitators or specialty welcome packages. These incentives add value without significantly impacting your bottom line.

Creating a Scholarship Program

A well-designed scholarship program can open doors for those who dream of attending your retreat but face financial barriers. Here's a framework for creating such a program:

- Define Criteria: Establish clear, fair criteria for scholarship eligibility. This might include financial need, contributions to their community, or how they plan to use the experience to make a difference.
- Funding Sources: Consider various funding sources for your scholarships. This might include allocating a portion of profits, seeking sponsorship from aligned businesses, or offering attendees a 'pay it forward' option to contribute.
- Application Process: Design a simple, dignified application process that allows candidates to share their stories and aspirations. Ensure this process respects their privacy and dignity, focusing on the potential impact of the scholarship.

Marketing Discounts and Scholarships

Effectively communicating about your discount and scholarship opportunities is crucial. It ensures those who stand to benefit most are aware and feel invited to apply. Here are some tips:

- Use Diverse Channels: Leverage your website, social media, email newsletters, and community partnerships to spread the word. Tailor your messaging to each platform to reach as broad and relevant an audience as possible.
- Highlight Stories: Share stories from past scholarship recipients or attendees who benefited from discounts. These testimonials can motivate potential applicants

and those considering contributing to the scholarship fund.

- Maintain Value Perception: Ensure that your communication emphasizes the value and transformative potential of the retreat. Discounts and scholarships should be framed as opportunities for inclusion, not as devaluations of the experience.

In weaving discounts and scholarships into the fabric of your retreat planning, you broaden the spectrum of individuals who can benefit from your offerings and enrich the tapestry of experiences and perspectives represented. It's a testament to the belief that personal growth and transformation should be accessible to all, regardless of financial circumstances. This approach amplifies the impact of your retreats and strengthens the community that forms around them, creating ripples of change that extend far beyond the confines of the retreat itself.

As we wrap up this exploration into the nuanced world of retreat pricing, it's clear that the artistry lies not in the numbers themselves but in how they're structured, communicated, and leveraged to create an experience that's both financially sustainable and profoundly inclusive. From understanding the foundational costs to creatively applying for discounts and scholarships, each element plays a crucial role in crafting retreats that welcome a vibrant mosaic of participants, each with their own stories, dreams, and contributions. This holistic approach to pricing is more than just a strategy; it reflects the values at the heart of your retreats—a commitment to accessibility, diversity, and transformation. As we turn our gaze to the horizon, let us carry forward these principles, knowing that the accurate measure of success lies in the lives touched and the communities built through the shared journey of discovery and growth.

CHAPTER 8

Managing the Flow: The Logistics of a Seamless Retreat

Have you ever seen a well-oiled machine? Every gear and cog working in perfect harmony, creating a powerful force that moves with precision and grace. This machine could be an elegant antique clock or a high-performance sports car. Still, in the world of retreats, the seamless orchestration of logistics sets the stage for transformative experiences. Just as a master chef knows that the secret to a perfect dish lies not just in the quality of the ingredients but in the meticulous preparation and timing, the success of a retreat hinges on the invisible yet crucial framework of logistics management. It's about ensuring that every detail, from arrival to departure, aligns to create an environment where transformation can flourish.

Checklists and Systems for Smooth Operations

Effective logistics management is the backbone of any successful retreat, acting as the invisible hand that guides the experience from behind the scenes. Several tools and strategies stand out as invaluable allies to ensure this process runs without a hitch.

- Comprehensive Checklists: A checklist is like a map in the wilderness; it shows you where you are, where you need to go, and what you need to get there. For retreat planning, this means having a detailed list for every phase of the retreat:
    - Pre-retreat Planning: This checklist covers all the tasks that must be completed before the retreat begins. It includes booking the venue, finalizing the schedule, confirming guest speakers or facilitators, and sending out pre-retreat information packets to attendees.
    - On-site Management: Once the retreat is underway, a different set of priorities emerges. This checklist keeps track of daily activities, meals, transportation logistics, and any special events or sessions. It also includes a quick-response plan for addressing immediate needs or unexpected issues.
    - Post-retreat Follow-up: The retreat experience doesn't end when participants go home. This checklist ensures that all post-retreat tasks are completed, such as gathering feedback, sending thank-you notes, and sharing resources or recordings from sessions.

- Project Management Software: In today's digital age, numerous tools can help streamline the coordination and communication of your organizing team. Platforms like Trello, Asana, or Monday.com allow you to assign tasks, track progress, and collaborate effectively, ensuring that nothing falls through the cracks.
- Delegating Responsibilities: A retreat is a symphony, and every organizing team member is an instrumentalist. Assigning clear roles and responsibilities is crucial:
    - Who: Identify who on your team is responsible for each task or area, such as logistics, content, participant engagement, etc.
    - What: Define what needs to be accomplished, giving detailed descriptions of each task or objective.
    - Where: Specify where these tasks will be carried out, whether at the retreat venue, off-site, or online.
    - When: Set deadlines for each task, ensuring a clear completion timeline.
    - Why: Understanding the purpose behind each task can help keep your team motivated and focused on the bigger picture.

Visual Element: Logistics Flowchart

A flowchart can be an excellent visual tool for mapping out the logistics of your retreat. It can illustrate the sequence of tasks, show dependencies between different planning areas, and highlight critical milestones. Consider creating a flowchart that covers the three main phases of retreat planning (pre-retreat, on-site, and post-retreat) and use color coding or symbols to designate different team members' responsibilities.

Interactive Element: Role Assignment Exercise
Try conducting a role assignment exercise to foster a sense of ownership and ensure that each team member is well-suited to their tasks. This can be done through a facilitated workshop or an online survey, where team members express their preferences and strengths. The goal is to match each person with the roles they are most excited about and capable of fulfilling, creating an effective and engaged team.

Effective logistics management is not just about ticking boxes and meeting deadlines; it's about creating a solid foundation upon which the magic of your retreat can unfold. By leveraging comprehensive checklists, harnessing the power of project management software, and thoughtfully delegating responsibilities, you set the stage for an experience that is as seamless as it is transformative. Remember, the smoother the logistics, the more participants can relax, engage, and open themselves up to the growth and change your retreat promises.

Handling Unexpected Challenges Gracefully

When leading a retreat, it's common to encounter surprises that test your adaptability and resilience. The key to navigating these waters smoothly lies in a blend of anticipation, preparation, and transparent communication.

Anticipate and Prepare for the Unexpected
The unexpected is, by nature, impossible to prepare for. However, a mindset geared towards flexibility allows you to anticipate a range of possibilities and prepare accordingly.

- Scenario Planning: Start by imagining various scenarios that could disrupt your retreat's smooth running. These might range from minor inconveniences like delayed supplies to more significant challenges such as sudden weather changes or health emergencies among participants. For each scenario, develop a plan that outlines specific steps to mitigate the impact.
- Resource Lists: Equally important is having a comprehensive list of resources readily available. This list should include contact information for local health services, emergency response teams, backup suppliers, and any other services you might need to call upon quickly. Knowing who to call and what to do can turn a potential crisis into a manageable situation.
- Flexibility in Scheduling: Build some flexibility into your retreat schedule. This could mean having backup sessions that don't require specific settings or materials, allowing for last-minute changes without leaving gaps in the itinerary. It's like keeping an extra card up your sleeve, ready to play if needed.

Leading with Calm and Decision
In moments of uncertainty, your participants will look to you for guidance and reassurance. How you handle

unexpected events can significantly influence the overall atmosphere of the retreat.

- Stay Informed: Keep yourself informed about any potential issues that could arise during the retreat, such as weather alerts or local events that might affect your plans. This ongoing awareness allows you to adjust plans proactively rather than reactively.
- Maintain Poise: When faced with an unexpected challenge, take a moment to breathe and center yourself before responding. This helps maintain a calm demeanor, reassuring participants that the situation is controlled, even if you're working out the details on the fly.
- Empower Your Team: Ensure that your team feels confident in their ability to handle unforeseen issues. This might mean delegating specific responsibilities or making quick decisions. A team that feels empowered is more likely to respond effectively to challenges, reducing the burden on you as the leader.

Transparent Communication with Participants

How you communicate with your participants during times of uncertainty can make a significant difference in their experience. Clear, honest communication helps manage expectations and build trust, even when things don't go as planned.

- Immediate and Clear Updates: If a situation affects the retreat schedule or activities, inform participants as soon as possible. Use clear and straightforward language to explain what has happened and how it will impact them. Avoid jargon or overly technical explanations, which can create more confusion.

- Offer Alternatives: Whenever possible, present participants with alternatives. If an outdoor activity is canceled due to weather, have an indoor alternative ready to suggest. This shows participants that you're prepared and committed to ensuring their experience is as enriching as possible despite any hiccups.
- Solicit Feedback: In some cases, involving participants in the decision-making process might be appropriate, especially if multiple alternatives are available. This can be as simple as taking a quick vote or having a brief discussion to gauge their preferences. Giving participants a say in handling situations can foster a sense of community and shared responsibility.

Unexpected challenges don't have to derail your retreat. With careful anticipation, the ability to maintain calm and make decisions, and a commitment to transparent communication, you can navigate these situations in a way that minimizes disruption and holds the trust and confidence of your participants. It's about embracing the unexpected as part of the journey, turning potential obstacles into opportunities for growth and learning for you and your participants.

Catering to Dietary and Accessibility Needs

Creating a space that feels welcoming to everyone is not just about the ambiance or the quality of sessions provided; it hinges significantly on how well we can accommodate the unique needs of each participant. This attention to detail, especially regarding dietary restrictions and physical accessibility, sends a powerful message about the inclusivity of your retreat.

Gathering and Accommodating Dietary Restrictions

In today's world, where dietary preferences and restrictions are as diverse as the individuals themselves, understanding and planning for these needs is not an option—it's a necessity. Here's how you can ensure everyone's dietary needs are met with care and consideration:

- Early Communication: Before the retreat begins, reach out to participants with a detailed form asking them to specify any dietary restrictions or preferences they might have. This could range from allergies and intolerances to lifestyle choices like veganism or ketogenic diets.
- Engage with Chefs and Caterers: Once you have collected this information, the next step involves a detailed discussion with your chefs or catering service. The goal is to ensure that for every meal, options are available that cater to the diverse needs of your participants. It's not just about having alternative dishes but ensuring these alternatives are equally thought-out and appealing.
- Label Foods Clearly: Provide clear, visible labels for every dish for buffets or shared meal settings. Labels should include ingredients and note common allergens. This practice allows participants to navigate

their options independently, making for a more comfortable and stress-free dining experience.

Assessing and Enhancing Venue Accessibility

A genuinely inclusive retreat goes beyond dietary accommodations; it ensures that all participants can navigate and enjoy the venue comfortably, regardless of physical ability. Here's a checklist to guide you in assessing and enhancing the physical accessibility of your retreat venue:

- Entrance and Common Areas: Ensure that all entry points and common areas are wheelchair accessible. This includes having ramps where necessary and ensuring doorways are wide enough to accommodate mobility aids.
- Accommodation and Facilities: Assess the lodging options and facilities for accessibility features such as bathroom grab bars, lower sink heights, and accessible shower options. If your venue does not meet these standards, work with them to find temporary solutions or consider alternative venues that better cater to these needs.
- Transport and Activities: For retreats that include off-site activities or require transportation, ensure that all modes of transport are accessible. Similarly, evaluate the accessibility of any external venues or activity sites being used as part of the retreat program.

Partnering with Inclusive Service Providers

The ethos of inclusivity should extend to every aspect of

your retreat, including the partners and service providers you choose to work with. Here are some tips for ensuring your partners share your commitment to accessibility and accommodation:

- Vet for Inclusivity: When selecting vendors, whether for catering, activities, or transportation, prioritize those with a proven track record of accommodating diverse needs. Ask potential partners about their experience and strategies for handling dietary restrictions and accessibility requirements.
- Collaborative Planning: Work closely with your partners to ensure they fully understand the specific needs of your participants. This might involve joint planning sessions or walkthroughs of the venue to discuss and plan for necessary accommodations.
- Feedback Loop: Create a system for gathering feedback from your partners and service providers during and after the retreat. This feedback can be invaluable in identifying areas for improvement and ensuring that your commitment to inclusivity is consistently upheld.

By strongly emphasizing meeting dietary restrictions and ensuring venue accessibility, you not only affirm the value of each participant but also foster an environment where diversity is celebrated and accommodated. This approach enhances the experience for those with specific needs and elevates the retreat experience for all attendees, creating a space where everyone can relax, engage, and transform without the worry of logistical hurdles.

The Role of Technology in Retreat Logistics

In orchestrating retreats, the infusion of technology has become a crucial element in enhancing both the efficiency of operations and participants' overall experience. This digital evolution touches every aspect of the retreat, from the initial sign-up process to the final farewells, ensuring that each step is as smooth and engaging as possible.

Streamlining Registration and Communication

The journey starts with the first click on the registration page. Here, technology acts as the gateway, making signing up for the retreat straightforward and inviting. Online registration platforms offer a suite of tools that go beyond simple form submissions. They allow for the integration of payment processing, automatic confirmation emails, and even personalized follow-up messages, ensuring that they feel welcomed and informed from the moment participants decide to join.

- Automated Emails: Setting up automated email sequences can significantly reduce the workload on the organizing team. From welcome emails to pre-retreat checklists and reminders, these communications keep participants in the loop and build anticipation for the retreat experience.
- Participant Portals: Offering participants access to an online portal can elevate their experience from the outset. Here, they can find detailed itineraries, packing lists, and forums to connect with fellow attendees.

This portal becomes a one-stop shop for all their retreat-related queries and discussions.

Mobile Apps: Keeping Participants Informed and Engaged
The power of smartphones can be harnessed to keep participants informed and engaged throughout the retreat. Creating a dedicated mobile app for the retreat can serve multiple functions, acting as a pocket-sized companion for every attendee.

- Personalized Schedules: Within the app, participants can access their personalized schedules, including session times, locations, and any optional activities they've signed up for. This feature ensures that everyone knows where they need to be and when reducing confusion and maximizing participation.
- Live Updates and Notifications: The dynamic nature of retreats means that sometimes, changes to the schedule are inevitable. A mobile app allows real-time updates and notifications to be sent directly to participants' phones, ensuring everyone is always up to date with the latest information.
- Interactive Maps: Interactive maps within the app can be invaluable for retreats spread across larger venues or those that include off-site excursions. Participants can easily navigate from one location to another, finding everything from session halls to dining areas with a simple tap on their screen.

Virtual Platforms: Extending the Retreat Experience
The conclusion of a retreat doesn't mean the end of the

journey. Virtual platforms offer an incredible opportunity to extend the retreat experience, maintaining the momentum of growth and community long after the last goodbye.

- Online Workshops and Sessions: Hosting follow-up workshops or sessions online allows for continued learning and development. These can be particularly beneficial for participants who wish to delve deeper into topics covered during the retreat or those looking for ongoing support in applying what they've learned to their daily lives.
- Community Forums: Creating an online community space where participants can share their experiences, challenges, and successes fosters a sense of belonging and support. These forums can be hosted on the retreat's website or through social media groups, providing a platform for ongoing connection and inspiration.
- Resource Libraries: Compiling resources, recordings of sessions, and other relevant materials in an online library allows participants to revisit the wisdom and insights shared during the retreat. This digital repository can become valuable for participants as they continue their personal and professional growth journeys.

Technology, when thoughtfully integrated into the fabric of retreat logistics, has the potential to transform the administrative landscape into one that is fluid, interactive, and deeply enriching. It bridges the gap between the practical necessities of organizing a retreat and the aspiration to create an experience that is memorable, impactful, and seamlessly executed. From the ease of registration to the depth of post-retreat engagement, technology plays a pivotal role in crafting retreats that resonate on every level, ensuring that each participant's journey is as fulfilling as it is unforgettable.

Post-Retreat Follow-Up: Maintaining Connections

After the final session ends and participants begin their journey home, the threads of connection woven during the retreat remain vibrant and vital. The challenge now lies in nurturing these bonds and continuing the momentum of growth and community that has been so carefully cultivated. The period following a retreat is not merely a time for reflection but an opportunity to extend the transformation and deepen the relationships formed. Here, we explore strategies that ensure the retreat's impact resonates well beyond its physical conclusion.

Gathering feedback is more than a procedural step; it invites participants to share their experiences, insights, and suggestions. This valuable information informs the planning of future retreats and makes participants feel heard and valued.

- Surveys with Heart: Design post-retreat surveys beyond logistics to ask about personal growth, moments of connection, and suggestions for deepening the experience. These surveys should feel personal and thoughtful, reflecting the spirit of the retreat.

- Conversations That Matter: In addition to structured surveys, informal conversations can reveal nuanced feedback and stories of transformation. Consider follow-up calls or video chats to connect more personally, offering a space for deeper reflection and sharing.
- The power of shared experiences to forge lasting bonds is immense. Creating spaces for continued connection ensures the retreat community remains active and supportive.
- Exclusive Online Groups: Launching a private forum or social media group for retreat participants creates a space for ongoing sharing, support, and inspiration. Here, members can post updates on their journey, share resources, and even organize local meetups.
- Virtual Gatherings: Regularly scheduled virtual meetups, such as group meditations, book discussions, or check-in sessions, keep the retreat spirit alive. These gatherings help maintain the sense of community and shared purpose established during the retreat.

The lessons and memories from the retreat are treasures to be revisited and cherished. Sharing resources, recordings, and photographs helps participants reconnect with their experience and integrate their learnings into daily life.

- Resource Sharing: Compile and share a digital package of retreat materials, including session recordings, reading lists, and guided meditations. This resource hub becomes a tool for ongoing learning and practice.
- Capturing Memories: A photo album or video montage of the retreat captures the essence of the experience in a way words cannot. Sharing this visual diary not only brings back fond memories but also serves as a reminder of the journey and the community that shared it.

As the chapter on post-retreat follow-up comes to a close, we reflect on the importance of maintaining the connections and momentum initiated during our time together.

Through thoughtful surveys, dedicated spaces for ongoing engagement, and the sharing of resources and memories, we ensure that the impact of the retreat experience continues to unfold in the lives of its participants. This approach not only enriches the personal journeys of each individual but also strengthens the collective fabric of the retreat community, setting the stage for future gatherings and shared growth. As we look ahead, we carry the lessons learned, and the connections forged, ready to weave them into the tapestry of our next adventure.

CHAPTER 9
Building a Thriving Retreat Portfolio

Envision sipping your favorite cup of coffee early in the morning, the air crisp and filled with possibilities. Now, think of this as not just a single day's pleasure but a ritual, evolving over seasons, each cup bringing its flavor, depth, and warmth. Similarly, hosting a retreat isn't a one-time affair. It's about creating a series, each with its unique essence yet part of a larger, enriching tradition. This chapter delves into transforming a single retreat into a thriving portfolio, attracting a wider audience, and ensuring your offerings remain fresh, relevant, and financially rewarding.

From One-off to Series: Building a Retreat Portfolio

Transitioning from hosting a single retreat to offering a series can attract a wider audience and increase revenue.

Crafting a series of retreats allows you to cater to your audience's various interests, learning curves, and availability schedules. Like a coffee aficionado experimenting with different beans and brew methods, diversifying your retreat themes and formats invites both novices and connoisseurs into your world. Here's how to make it happen:

- Identify Themes and Formats: Start with what you know. Look at the feedback from your initial retreat(s). What themes resonated the most? Were there requests for deeper dives into specific topics? Use this data to draft a list of potential themes. Consider varying formats, too; weekend workshops, week-long immersions, or even day retreats offer flexibility to your audience.

- Leverage Success and Feedback: Every retreat teaches something new about your audience, content, and yourself. Use this goldmine of insights to refine your offerings. Perhaps the silent meditation sessions were a hit, or the creative writing workshops filled up fast. Use these cues to shape your future retreats, ensuring each series builds on the success of the last.

- Create a Cohesive Brand Experience: Consistency in quality, ethos, and aesthetics across your retreats fosters brand loyalty. Your participants should feel a familiar warmth and welcome, whether attending a retreat focused on mindfulness, creative expression, or personal development. Yet, ensure each event stands out with its unique offerings and surprises. It's about striking the right balance between the known's comfort and the new's excitement.

Visual Element: Portfolio Roadmap

An infographic that visually represents the roadmap for your retreat portfolio can be incredibly insightful. The roadmap could outline potential themes for the year, showing how each retreat builds upon the last and highlighting special formats or locations. This visual tool not only aids in your planning but can also be shared with your audience, giving them a glimpse of what's ahead and building anticipation.

Interactive Element: Theme Voting

Engage your audience in the creation process by hosting a theme voting session. This could be done through an online poll where past and potential participants vote on the themes they're most interested in exploring next. This fosters a sense of community and inclusion and gives you direct insight into your audience's preferences, helping you tailor your portfolio to match their interests.

Textual Element: Case Studies of Successful Series

Include detailed case studies of retreat series that have seen success. For instance, a wellness coach launched a "Seasons of Self-Care" series, offering a different retreat with each change of season, each focusing on what self-care looks like in the context of the season's challenges and opportunities. These case studies can serve as inspiration and a blueprint for what might work within your retreat series.

Transitioning to a series-based approach in hosting retreats opens a world of possibilities. It allows for deeper exploration of themes, caters to varying participant needs, and creates a sustainable business model. Each retreat becomes a chapter in a larger story you're telling, one that invites people back, time and again, to discover more about the topics you're passionate about and, ultimately, more about themselves.

Leveraging Online Retreats and Workshops

The digital age has transformed how we connect, learn, and grow together. With the click of a button, we can open doors to new experiences from the comfort of our homes. This reality brings to light the potential of online retreats and workshops. These virtual gatherings can extend the reach of your message, making transformative experiences accessible to a global audience. Yet, venturing into the digital realm comes with its unique set of challenges and opportunities.

Online retreats can significantly reduce overhead costs associated with physical venues, travel, and accommodations. This financial advantage allows for a more flexible pricing model, making your offerings accessible to a broader audience. However, the absence of a physical space means you must find innovative ways to create engaging and immersive content that captivates your participants through their screens.

Creating interactive and immersive online experiences demands a blend of creativity and technology. Here are some strategies to ensure your virtual retreats are just as impactful as their in-person counterparts:

- Engage Through Storytelling: Use the power of storytelling to create a narrative that participants can connect with. Share stories that resonate with your audience's experiences, challenges, and aspirations. This approach can help break down the digital barrier, making the online environment more personal and engaging.
- Interactive Sessions: Incorporate interactive elements into your sessions to foster engagement and participation. This can include live Q&A segments, breakout rooms for small group discussions, and interactive polls. These elements encourage active participation, making attendees feel involved and invested in the experience.
- Visual and Audio Enhancements: Use high-quality visuals and audio to enrich your presentations. Beautiful imagery, soothing background music, and clear, crisp sound can elevate the online experience, making it more enjoyable and professional.
- Personal Connection: Allocate time for personal check-ins and sharing. Create spaces where participants can share their reflections, challenges, and breakthroughs. This can be facilitated through dedicated sharing sessions or by incorporating reflection prompts that participants can respond to in chat or breakout rooms.

Choosing the right technology platforms and tools is crucial for facilitating seamless virtual retreats. Consider the following when making your selection:

- User-Friendliness: Opt for intuitive and easy-to-navigate platforms for both you and your participants. The less time spent troubleshooting technical issues, the more time can be devoted to the retreat experience.
- Interactive Features: Look for interactive platforms such as breakout rooms, chat functions, and polling. These features can make your virtual retreat more dynamic and engaging.
- Reliability and Support: Choose reliable platforms that offer robust customer support. This ensures that any technical issues can be quickly addressed, minimizing disruptions to your retreat.
- Integration Capabilities: Platforms that allow for integrating other tools and apps can enhance the functionality of your virtual retreat. Whether it's incorporating a registration system, payment gateway, or social media, these integrations can streamline the experience for both organizers and participants.

Implementing these strategies can help you create virtual retreats and workshops that not only mirror the transformational impact of in-person events but also offer unique benefits. I've asked online participants to come to a virtual retreat with their favorite scent, flavor, and song. They were able to incorporate these tools when asked to in various exercises I'd planned.

With careful planning, a creative approach, and the right technology, you can craft online experiences that leave a lasting impression on your participants, no matter where they are in the world.

Building a Community of Repeat Attendees

Creating a community that continually returns for your retreats is akin to nurturing a garden. It requires attention, care, and the right conditions to flourish. This section delves into the methods you can employ to cultivate such a community, ensuring your retreats remain vibrant with familiar faces and new ones brought in by the allure of your growing reputation.

Engaging Past Participants with Exclusive Offers and Updates

Keeping the flame of interest alive in those who have previously attended your retreats is crucial. These individuals have already experienced the value you provide and are, therefore, more likely to return if reminded of the benefits and given the right incentives.

- Early Access: Give past attendees first dibs on upcoming retreats before they're announced to the broader public. This makes them feel valued and increases the likelihood of their early commitment.
- Special Discounts: Offer discounts exclusive to returning attendees. A tangible reward for their loyalty can significantly boost repeat attendance.
- Updates and Newsletters: Regular updates keep your retreats top of mind for past attendees. Through engaging newsletters, share exciting developments,

upcoming retreat themes, and personal stories or testimonials that highlight the transformative experiences at your retreats.

Rewarding Repeat Attendance and Referrals

Loyalty and referral programs can be powerful incentives, encouraging repeat attendance and bringing new participants into the fold through word-of-mouth recommendations.

- Loyalty Programs: Implement a points system where attendees accumulate points for each retreat they attend. These points could then be redeemed for discounts, special perks, or exclusive experiences in future retreats.

- Referral Rewards: Encourage and reward past attendees for referring friends or family members. Offer both the referrer and the referred a discount or a special gift as a token of appreciation. This increases your retreat's visibility and strengthens the community by bringing in like-minded individuals.

Personalized Communication and Feedback Loops

In a world often dominated by mass marketing and impersonal communication, taking the time to personalize your interactions can set you apart and forge deeper connections with your participants.

- Personal Notes: Send personalized thank-you notes or emails after a retreat. Acknowledge their participation and share a memorable moment or insight from the retreat. This personal touch can make attendees feel seen and appreciated.

- Feedback Surveys: Invite honest feedback through post-retreat surveys. Ask specific questions to gauge what attendees loved and what could be improved. Show that you value their opinions by actively incorporating their suggestions into future retreat planning.

- Birthday and Special Occasion Messages: Record attendees' birthdays or other significant dates they may share during the retreat. Sending a thoughtful message or a small gift on these special occasions can reinforce their emotional connection to your community.

Interactive Element: Community Building Workshops
Host online or in-person workshops focusing on community building amongst past and potential retreat attendees. These workshops can cover topics relevant to your retreat's theme but should emphasize interactive and collaborative activities that foster connections among participants. For instance, a collaborative storytelling workshop allows attendees to share and listen to each other's stories and builds a sense of community and shared experience.

Textual Element: The Story Behind Our Community
Share the evolution of your retreat community through stories and testimonials in a dedicated section of your website or newsletter. Highlight attendees' journeys who

have become regulars, showcasing their growth and the community's role in their lives. This narrative humanizes your brand and illustrates the tangible benefits of becoming a part of your community.

Building a community of repeat attendees is about creating a sense of belonging and value. It's about recognizing and rewarding loyalty, engaging in meaningful, personalized communication, and providing platforms for connections to deepen. Through these efforts, you establish more than just a recurring revenue stream; you cultivate a thriving community that supports and enriches your brand and its individuals.

Partnerships and Sponsorships for Growth

In the realm of retreat planning, joining forces with like-minded businesses and individuals can elevate the experience for your participants and broaden the horizons of your offerings. These collaborations can inject your retreats with fresh ideas, additional resources, and even new audiences. Here's how you can navigate the waters of partnerships and sponsorships to enrich your retreats and extend their reach.

Finding the Right Partners and Sponsors

The first step is identifying potential partners and sponsors that resonate with your retreat's mission and values. This alignment is key to ensuring that collaboration adds genuine value to your retreats without compromising their integrity. Start by listing companies, local businesses, or individual entrepreneurs who serve a similar demographic or share your commitment to personal growth, wellness, or whatever niche your retreat occupies.

- Look for businesses that offer products or services that could enhance the retreat experience, such as wellness brands, local artisans, or even tech companies with tools that support mindfulness and productivity.
- Consider the audience overlap. Partners whose audiences closely mirror or complement your own are more likely to be beneficial collaborators.
- Reach out with a well-thought-out proposition that clearly outlines the mutual benefits of the partnership. Highlight how the collaboration could offer them access to a new, engaged audience and enhance their brand visibility.

Negotiating Mutually Beneficial Agreements
Once you've identified potential partners or sponsors, the next step is to craft agreements that serve both parties well. This negotiation process is crucial and should be approached with a clear understanding of what you can offer and what you hope to gain.

- Be upfront about your expectations and open to hearing what your potential partners seek in the collaboration. This could range from brand exposure at your event to content creation that features their products or services.

- Discuss the specifics of the collaboration, such as whether they'll provide financial sponsorship, products for participants, or services like catering or tech support for online retreats.
- Determine the metrics of success for both sides. Will success be measured by participant engagement, social media exposure, or some other metric? Agreeing on these terms upfront can help prevent misunderstandings down the line.

Integrating Partners and Sponsors Into the Retreat Experience

With the right partners and sponsors on board, the focus shifts to seamlessly integrating their contributions into your retreats in a way that enhances the participant experience. This integration should feel organic and aligned with the retreat's theme and goals.

- For product-based collaborations, consider creative ways to incorporate these products into the retreat. This could be through welcome packs that include items from your sponsors, using sponsored goods as tools or materials in your sessions, or setting up a pop-up shop where participants can explore the products first-hand.
- For service-based sponsorships, consider how these services can add value to the retreat. A tech company might offer a workshop on digital wellness, or a local farm could provide a farm-to-table dining experience.

- Always keep the participant experience at the forefront of your planning. Every sponsored element should feel like an enhancement, not an interruption. Avoid overt sales pitches or anything that feels out of place with the retreat's ethos.

Showcasing Your Partners and Sponsors

Recognizing your partners and sponsors before, during, and after the retreat is crucial for maintaining strong relationships and showing appreciation for their support. There are several ways to do this effectively.

- In your promotional materials, highlight your partners and sponsors, explaining their role in the retreat and how they're contributing to the experience. This can be done through social media shout-outs, newsletter features, or mentions in your press releases.
- During the retreat, ensure there are moments where your partners' contributions are acknowledged. This could be through signage at the event, verbal shout-outs during sessions, or dedicated time for partners to share their stories or missions with participants.
- After the retreat, share the success with your partners and sponsors. Please provide them with metrics of engagement, photographs of their products or services in action, and testimonials from participants that underscore the value they added. This not only shows appreciation but also strengthens the relationship for future collaborations.

In the end, partnerships and sponsorships offer a powerful avenue for growth, innovation, and enhanced participant experience in your retreat business. By carefully selecting partners that align with your mission, negotiating agreements that benefit both sides, and thoughtfully integrating their contributions, you can create richer, more diverse, and even more impactful retreats.

Evaluating Success and Planning for the Future

In the dynamic landscape of hosting retreats, the close of one event marks the starting point for reflection and forward thinking. It's a cycle of learning, adapting, and evolving to meet your audience's ever-changing needs while expanding your reach. This continuous loop of evaluation and planning ensures your retreats remain relevant and thrive in a competitive market.

Setting Benchmarks Beyond the Balance Sheet

While financial viability is a critical measure of success, the true value of a retreat extends into realms less tangible but equally vital. Participant satisfaction, personal growth outcomes, and the strength of the community forged during your retreat offer insights into its deeper impact.

- Participant Satisfaction: Gauging the happiness and satisfaction of your attendees is crucial. Surveys and one-on-one conversations post-retreat can reveal much about what worked and what didn't, offering a clear direction for future improvements.

- Personal Transformations: Observing and documenting the personal growth of participants provides a qualitative measure of success. Encourage attendees to share their stories of transformation, whether through written testimonials, video diaries, or social media posts.
- Community Engagement: The vibrancy of the community that emerges from your retreats speaks volumes about their success. Monitor the activity within online forums, follow-up events, and the frequency of peer-to-peer interactions as indicators of a thriving community.

Framework for Post-Retreat Evaluation

A systematic approach to post-retreat evaluation ensures no stone is left unturned in understanding the multifaceted success of your event. This framework involves gathering feedback from all stakeholders involved.

- Participant Feedback: Utilize surveys that probe beyond surface-level reactions to delve into the specifics of the retreat experience, from logistics and content to personal outcomes and future intentions.
- Staff and Partner Insights: The perspectives of your team and any partners or sponsors involved can offer valuable insights into areas for improvement and potential growth opportunities.
- Performance Against Objectives: Review the goals set for the retreat and assess performance against these objectives. This evaluation should consider

quantitative targets, such as attendance numbers, and qualitative goals, such as participant engagement.

Leveraging Insights for Strategic Planning

The insights from a thorough evaluation process are gold dust for strategic planning. They inform immediate adjustments and long-term strategies for scaling and evolving your retreat offerings.

- Identifying Opportunities: Look for patterns in feedback that suggest new themes, formats, or markets to explore. Participant suggestions can often spark innovative ideas for future retreats.
- Adapting to Market Trends: Stay attuned to shifts in the broader market landscape. Evaluation insights can help you anticipate participant preferences changes, emerging interest themes, or new competitive challenges.
- Strategic Scaling: Use evaluation data to make informed decisions about scaling your retreat business. This might involve expanding your retreat portfolio, exploring new locations, or increasing the frequency of events.

In essence, the cycle of evaluating success and planning for the future is about staying agile and responsive to your audience's explicit and implicit needs. It's about more than just sustaining your business; it's about ensuring that every retreat you host carries the seeds of growth, transformation, and community. Through diligent analysis and strategic foresight, you can continue to create retreat experiences that resonate deeply with participants, fostering an environment where personal breakthroughs are not just possible but expected.

As we wrap up this discussion, it's clear that the journey of hosting retreats is a continuous learning process that requires us to listen, adapt, and innovate. The insights gathered from each event feed into the next, ensuring that every retreat is a step forward in offering more value, deeper transformations, and stronger connections. This cycle of evaluation and planning not only sets the stage for the sustainable growth of your retreat business and ensures that the experiences you create remain impactful and relevant in an ever-evolving world. With this foundation, we move forward, ready to explore new horizons and create retreats that continue to inspire and transform lives.

CHAPTER 10:
Riding the Wave of Retreat Innovation

One final time, imagine yourself sitting at a café, overhearing conversations from the next table. One group discusses a retreat that blends yoga with cutting-edge wellness technology, sparking curiosity. Another group reminisces about its last eco-conscious retreat that minimized its carbon footprint and involved the local community. These snippets of conversations are not just idle chatter; they are signposts pointing toward the evolving landscape of retreats.

Much like a kaleidoscope, the retreat industry shifts and turns, revealing new patterns and possibilities. Staying ahead or keeping pace requires an ear to the ground and an open mind to adapt and innovate. Here, we explore emerging trends shaping the future of retreats, offering insights on how to weave these trends into your offerings seamlessly.

Emerging Trends in the Retreat Industry

The retreat industry is witnessing a fascinating evolution, with emerging trends catering to the growing demand for wellness, technology integration, and environmental consciousness. Understanding these trends is not just about adding new bells and whistles to your retreats; it's about aligning with participants' shifting desires and expectations.

- Wellness Technology: The rise of wearable tech and wellness apps is not new, but integrating these into retreats is a burgeoning trend. Consider offering sessions where participants learn to use wellness apps effectively or incorporating wearable tech to monitor stress levels during meditation sessions. This adds a modern twist and empowers participants with tools they can use long after the retreat ends.

- Eco-conscious Retreats: With a growing awareness of environmental issues, participants seek retreats that walk the talk on sustainability. This could mean choosing venues that practice waste reduction and energy efficiency to including activities that teach participants about local conservation efforts. The key here is to minimize the environmental impact and weave the ethos of sustainability into the retreat experience.

- Hybrid Virtual/In-Person Formats: The pandemic accelerated the adoption of virtual gatherings, and the retreat industry is no exception. Hybrid models, where participants can choose to join in person or virtually, offer flexibility and inclusivity. Imagine a retreat where virtual participants join via live stream for meditation sessions or workshops, ensuring no one misses out due to travel constraints or health concerns.

Visual Element: Trend Infographic

An infographic that visually maps out these trends, highlighting key statistics, participant testimonials, and practical tips for integration, can be a valuable tool. It not only serves as a quick reference guide but also as an inspiration for how to bring these trends to life in your retreats.

Conducting Market Research to Gather Insights

Staying updated with industry trends requires a proactive approach to market research. This involves:

- Attending Industry Conferences: These gatherings are goldmines of information, offering insights into what's new and next. They're also great for networking with peers and learning from their experiences.
- Surveying Past Participants: Your best resource might be your past participants. A survey asking about their interests, feedback on past retreats, and what they'd like to see in the future can provide direct insights into evolving preferences.
- Social Media and Online Forums: Platforms like Instagram, Reddit, and specialized wellness forums are where many enthusiasts share their retreat experiences and desires. Monitoring these platforms

can offer a grassroots look at emerging trends and participant expectations.

Tips for Incorporating New Trends

Adding new trends to your retreat offerings requires a careful balance. It's not about overhauling your entire program but integrating elements that enhance the experience and align with your brand. Here are some tips:

- Start Small: Test the waters with small-scale integrations. For instance, introduce a session on eco-friendly living in your next retreat before planning an entirely eco-conscious retreat.
- Participant Feedback: Use feedback mechanisms to gauge participant response to these new elements. This helps fine-tune the integration and engages your participants in the evolution of your retreats.
- Collaborate with Experts: Collaborate with experts for areas outside your expertise, such as wellness technology or environmental conservation. This ensures the authenticity of the information shared and enriches the retreat experience with specialized knowledge.

Riding the wave of innovation in the retreat industry means being open to change and ready to adapt. It's about listening to the shifts in participant expectations and responding with relevant, impactful offerings, and aligned with your brand values. By staying informed about emerging trends and thoughtfully incorporating them into your retreats, you position yourself as a forward-thinking leader in the industry, ready to meet the needs and desires of tomorrow's participants.

Integrating Technology without Losing the Human Touch

In a world where screens often mediate our experiences, the question isn't whether to use technology in retreats but how to amplify rather than detract from the personal connections and transformative experiences at their core. The role of technology in enhancing the logistical framework, learning opportunities, and participant engagement of a retreat is undeniable. Yet, the careful selection and application of these technological tools ensure they bolster rather than overshadow the human elements that make retreats so powerful.

At the heart of any retreat lies the promise of personal transformation and deepened connections. When thoughtfully integrated, technology can be a powerful ally in this process. Here are some ways technology can complement the human aspects of a retreat, ensuring that participants leave feeling more connected to themselves and each other, not just to Wi-Fi.

- Digital Detox Zones: Amidst the tech-enhanced activities, designate areas or times where digital devices are encouraged to be put away. These zones encourage participants to connect with their surroundings and fellow attendees on a deeper level, fostering mindfulness and presence.

- App-based Mindfulness Challenges: Utilize apps to introduce daily mindfulness or gratitude challenges for participants. These can be done individually but shared within a group setting, using technology to spark personal reflection that's then enriched through group discussion.
- Virtual Icebreakers: Before the retreat begins, use online platforms to introduce participants to each other. Simple video introductions or digital games can break down initial barriers, making the first in-person meeting feel like a reunion of old friends.
- Tech-facilitated Learning: Incorporate technology to enhance learning experiences without making it the focal point. For example, use augmented reality (AR) to bring historical or cultural insights into a yoga practice held at an archaeological site, adding depth to the experience without detracting from the physical and mental practice.
- Social Media for Social Good: Encourage the use of social media in a way that fosters community and shared learning. A private group where participants can post reflections, photos, or insights encourages a different kind of engagement, one that's focused on sharing and connection rather than consumption.

In finding the balance between technology and personal touch, consider these guidelines:

- Purpose Over Novelty: Every piece of technology used should have a clear purpose that aligns with the retreat's goals. It's not about using tech for tech's sake but about enhancing the experience meaningfully.

- Accessibility and Ease of Use: Ensure that any tech incorporated is accessible to all participants, regardless of their familiarity with digital tools. Simple, intuitive solutions are often the most effective in bridging the gap between technology and personal experience.
- Feedback Loops: After introducing a new tech element, seek feedback. This will help you gauge whether it enhanced the experience or if adjustments are needed to ensure it adds value without overwhelming the human elements.

By weaving technology into the fabric of retreats with intention and care, we can create experiences that tap into the best of both worlds: the efficiency and innovation of the digital age, coupled with the timeless power of human connection and personal transformation. This thoughtful integration ensures that we lose neither the essence of retreats nor the invaluable human touch that defines them as we move forward.

Sustainability and Eco-Friendly Practices

In a world where the health of our planet is increasingly on everyone's mind, the retreat industry finds itself at a pivotal point. The choice to adopt sustainable and eco-friendly practices isn't just a nod to environmental responsibility; it's a response to a growing expectation from participants keen to see their values reflected in the events they attend. This shift towards sustainability isn't merely about reducing harm but about actively contributing to preserving and enhancing our natural world.

The significance of sustainability within the retreat space cannot be understated. Retreats offer a unique platform to practice environmental stewardship and educate and inspire participants to integrate these practices into their daily lives. From selecting eco-conscious venues to incorporating conservation activities, retreats can serve as catalysts for raising awareness and fostering a deeper connection to the environment.

For retreat organizers, the journey towards sustainability begins with conscious decision-making across all aspects of retreat planning. Here are key areas to consider:

- Location Choices: Opt for venues that prioritize sustainability in their operations. This could mean establishments that utilize renewable energy sources practice water conservation and implement waste reduction measures. The location can also play a part; natural settings can heighten participants' connection to the environment and underscore the importance of conservation efforts.
- Eco-conscious Supplies: Evaluate the materials and supplies used during your retreat. Every choice can contribute to a smaller ecological footprint from biodegradable yoga mats to reusable water bottles and eco-friendly name badges. Additionally, consider digital alternatives to printed materials, reducing

paper waste without sacrificing accessibility to information.

- Sustainable Dining: Food is a central component of most retreats and presents a significant opportunity to embrace sustainability. Collaborate with local farmers and suppliers to offer organic, plant-based meals that minimize environmental impact and support the local economy. This approach reduces carbon emissions associated with transportation and offers participants fresh, nutrient-rich dining options.

- Green Transportation: Encourage shared transportation options for participants traveling to the retreat venue. Whether arranging a shared shuttle service or promoting public transportation routes, reducing the number of vehicles on the road can significantly lower the event's carbon footprint. For more remote locations, consider offsetting carbon emissions by investing in renewable energy projects or reforestation efforts.

Communicating your commitment to sustainability is as important as the efforts themselves. Transparency about your practices not only educates participants but also fosters a sense of collective responsibility. Here's how you can effectively share your sustainability journey:

- Pre-Retreat Communication: Use your website, social media channels, and email correspondence to inform potential and registered participants about the eco-friendly aspects of your retreat. Detailing your sustainability measures can inspire participants to adopt similar practices in their travel preparations and daily lives.

- During the Retreat: Integrate discussions and activities on environmental conservation into your retreat schedule. Workshops on sustainable living guided nature walks focusing on local flora and fauna, and even participation in local conservation projects can enrich the retreat experience. These activities educate and empower participants to become advocates for the environment.

- Feedback and Involvement: Invite participants to contribute ideas for making the retreat more sustainable. This could be through suggestion boxes, dedicated brainstorming sessions, or post-retreat surveys. Participant input can provide valuable insights for enhancing your sustainability efforts and can foster a collaborative atmosphere where everyone feels invested in the retreat's environmental impact.

The adoption of sustainable and eco-friendly practices in the retreat industry represents more than a trend; it reflects a collective desire to protect and preserve our planet for future generations. Retreat organizers can significantly reduce their events' environmental impact by making mindful choices about locations, supplies, food, and transportation. More so, by openly communicating these efforts and involving participants in eco-friendly activities, retreats can become powerful platforms for promoting environmental awareness and conservation. In this way, retreats offer participants a chance for personal growth and renewal and contribute to the larger cause of sustainability, echoing the sentiment that every action, no matter how small, can make a difference.

The Evolving Needs of Tomorrow's Attendees

In the ever-shifting landscape of retreats, understanding attendees' evolving needs and preferences is not just beneficial—it's vital for any retreat to maintain its relevance and competitive edge. The tapestry of societal shifts, demographic changes, and the maturation of cultural expectations paints a picture of an audience that craves experiences that are not only transformative but also deeply respectful and inclusive of diverse perspectives.

Adapting to Societal and Demographic Shifts

The profile of retreat attendees is becoming more varied, reflecting broader societal and demographic changes. This diversity isn't just in age or geography but extends to life experiences, cultural backgrounds, and even expectations from the retreat experience itself. To stay ahead, retreat organizers must tune into these shifts, adapting their offerings to meet a wider array of needs and desires.

- Tailored Experiences: Gone are the days of one-size-fits-all retreats. Today's attendees expect experiences that cater to their specific life phase, whether young professionals seeking a break from the digital overload or older participants looking to explore new passions post-retirement.
- Flexibility: The ability to choose from various activities, varying in intensity and focus, allows

attendees to customize their experience. This flexibility can make a retreat appealing to a wider audience, from those seeking quiet reflection to others craving more dynamic, physically challenging activities.

Fostering Inclusivity and Cultural Sensitivity
Creating an environment where every attendee feels welcomed and valued is key to a successful retreat. This means going beyond acknowledging diversity to actively creating experiences that are inclusive and culturally sensitive.

- Language and Communication: Use inclusive language and avoid assumptions about participants' backgrounds, preferences, or abilities. Providing materials in multiple languages or offering translation services can significantly affect how participants engage with the retreat.
- Cultural Awareness: Incorporate elements that reflect and respect the cultural diversity of attendees. This could involve celebrating cultural traditions, offering a variety of cuisines, or including practices from different spiritual traditions respectfully.
- Accessibility: Ensure that venues are accessible to people with disabilities and consider the needs of those with dietary restrictions, health conditions, or other special requirements. Making everyone feel physically comfortable and accommodated is a foundational step in creating an inclusive retreat environment.

Leveraging Feedback for Continuous Improvement

The key to adapting to the evolving needs of retreat attendees lies in actively seeking and thoughtfully analyzing their feedback. This continuous loop of feedback and refinement helps keep your retreats aligned with participant expectations and emerging trends.

- Direct Surveys: Conduct surveys that ask pointed questions about attendees' experiences, preferences, and suggestions for future retreats. Digital platforms can facilitate immediate and anonymous responses, encouraging honesty and detailed feedback.
- Observation and Informal Conversations: Sometimes, the most insightful feedback comes from casual conversations or observing participants during the retreat. These observations can reveal unspoken needs or preferences that formal surveys might miss.
- Analyzing Trends: Combine the feedback from individual retreats with broader market research to identify overarching trends in retreat attendance. Tools like sentiment analysis on social media posts or trend analysis in search queries can provide valuable insights into what potential attendees are looking for.

Strategies for Meeting Evolving Needs

Meeting the changing needs of tomorrow's attendees requires a proactive and strategic approach. Here are some strategies that can help retreat organizers stay ahead of the curve:

- Continuous Learning and Education: Staying informed about cultural trends, wellness innovations, and teaching methodologies can inspire new retreat concepts that resonate with emerging attendee profiles.
- Collaboration and Partnerships: Working with experts from different fields, cultures, or disciplines can bring fresh perspectives and unique offerings to your retreats. These collaborations can also help in ensuring cultural sensitivity and inclusivity.
- Pilot Programs and Beta Retreats: Before rolling out significant changes or new themes, consider hosting pilot retreats or beta versions to gather direct feedback. This allows for real-world testing of new concepts with a smaller, perhaps more targeted audience.

As we navigate the complexities of an ever-evolving audience, the key lies in our ability to listen, adapt, and innovate. The future of retreats promises to be as diverse and dynamic as the attendees, offering endless opportunities for growth, learning, and connection. By staying attuned to our participants' changing needs and preferences, we ensure the continued relevance of our retreats and their ability to inspire and transform lives in meaningful ways.

Leaving a Legacy Through Your Retreats

Creating retreats that resonate deeply with attendees is

about more than providing a temporary sanctuary from the world's hustle. It's about planting seeds of change that grow and spread long after the final farewell. This legacy, a blend of personal transformation, strengthened connections, and positive contributions to communities, becomes the enduring heartbeat of your retreats.

The Ripple Effect of Transformation
Every retreat has the potential to alter the course of someone's life. Participants arrive with unique stories and leave with new chapters waiting to unfold. This transformation goes beyond the individual, rippling out to touch the lives of those around them.

- Stories of attendees who, inspired by a wellness retreat, lead healthier lifestyles, influencing their families and friends to do the same.
- Participants who discover a newfound confidence in a writing retreat, leading them to publish works that inspire and move others.
- Individuals who, after experiencing the power of mindful living, introduce practices in their workplaces, creating calm ripples in previously high-stress environments.

These transformations are the legacy of your retreats, testimonies to the profound impact that carefully curated experiences can have on individuals and, by extension, on their communities.

Social Impact Initiatives: Extending the Reach

A retreat can serve as a catalyst for positive change internally for the participants and externally in the wider community. Integrating social impact initiatives into your retreats can bridge the gap between personal development and community contribution.

- Partnering with local non-profits to include a day of service as part of the retreat, where attendees contribute to projects like reforestation, educational programs, or community beautification.
- Launching fundraising efforts during the retreat to support causes aligned with the retreat's theme, such as mental health resources or environmental conservation groups.
- Creating platforms for participants to continue supporting these initiatives post-retreat through donations, volunteer work, or spreading awareness.

These actions extend the legacy of your retreat to tangible contributions that benefit others, reinforcing the idea that personal growth and social responsibility can go hand in hand.

Fostering Lasting Connections and Communities

The potential to forge deep, meaningful connections is at the heart of every retreat. These bonds, built on shared experiences and mutual growth, often outlast the retreat, becoming sources of support, inspiration, and collaboration.

- Establishing alum networks that keep participants connected long after the retreat ends, providing a space for continued support and sharing.
- Organizing reunions or follow-up retreats for past participants, fostering a sense of ongoing community and offering opportunities for further growth.
- Encouraging and facilitating participant-led projects or groups that emerge from shared interests discovered during the retreat, be it a collaborative art project, a business venture, or a community service initiative.

This ongoing community building ensures that the legacy of your retreats includes not just individual transformations but the creation of vibrant, supportive networks that span the globe.

Envisioning Retreats with a Legacy Mindset
Designing retreats that leave a lasting positive impact requires intentionality from the outset. It's about seeing beyond the immediate experience to the potential for long-term growth and contribution. Here's how you can approach this:

- Start clarifying the values and outcomes you want your retreat to embody and promote. This vision guides every decision, from the choice of activities to the selection of partners and sponsors.
- Incorporate elements that encourage reflection on the retreat's broader impact, such as discussions on how

participants can apply what they've learned in their communities or create positive change in their environments.

- Provide resources and support for participants to keep the momentum going post-retreat, whether through online platforms, ongoing coaching, or connections to local initiatives aligned with the retreat's themes.

This perspective shifts the focus from creating a singular, memorable event to building a movement, one retreat at a time. Read that sentence again and really take it in!

In wrapping up, it's clear that the true measure of a retreat's success lies not just in the immediate feedback or the visible transformations during the event. It's found in the stories that unfold in the weeks, months, and years that follow—stories of personal breakthroughs turned into actions, connections that blossom into lifelong friendships, and small ripples that grow into waves of positive change. This legacy, built on the foundation of meaningful experiences and intentional community engagement, truly defines the impact of your retreats.

Moving forward, let's carry this legacy mindset with us, crafting each retreat as an isolated event and a steppingstone towards a larger vision of transformation and contribution.

Conclusion

As we draw the curtains on this remarkable journey together, it's essential to take a moment and reflect on the ground we've covered. From the foundational stones of hosting successful retreats to navigating the intricacies of scaling and innovating within this vibrant industry, our journey has been nothing short of transformative. Together, we've explored the potent magic that experiential retreats wield—a magic potent enough to catalyze business growth, foster profound personal development, and deepen the connections we share with our clients and participants. These experiences are more than just events; they are powerful vessels of transformation for hosts and attendees.

Throughout this book, we've delved into the essence of creating impactful retreats. We've unraveled the significance of aligning our retreat visions with our core values, the art of intimately understanding our audience and the importance of crafting agendas that speak to the heart of transformation. We've discussed the nuances of selecting the perfect locale, the dynamics of effective marketing, and the strategies for pricing that ensure success. We've navigated the logistical challenges and embraced the potential for scaling our retreat business while keeping our sights set on the dual impact these retreats have on personal and professional development.

As you stand on the threshold of this exciting venture, please take that bold first step toward hosting your own retreat. Let the insights and strategies shared in these pages be your guide to creating experiences that resonate deeply and leave a lasting impact. Remember, every challenge encountered along the way is an opportunity for growth, an invitation to innovate and redefine what's possible in your retreat offerings.

Looking ahead, envision a future where retreats serve as pivotal platforms for business development and as sanctuaries for personal transformation and healing. This future is within your grasp. Stay informed, remain adaptable, and continuously seek ways to elevate your retreat experiences, ensuring they remain vibrant and meaningful in an ever-evolving landscape.

Moreover, let's remember the profound legacy these retreats can foster. Beyond the immediate enrichment and financial benefits, consider how your retreats can contribute to broader causes, build communities, and leave a mark that transcends time. The impact of your work has the potential to ripple through lives, creating a legacy of transformation and connection.

Remember, continuous learning, adaptation, and innovation are the key to thriving in the retreat industry. This book is but a gateway to endless possibilities—embrace new ideas, welcome feedback, and keep your heart open to the ever-changing tides of this industry.

Lastly, I extend my deepest gratitude for allowing me to join your journey. You're not alone in this quest to create transformative retreat experiences. The journey, with its highs and lows, is as rewarding as the destination. May you find fulfillment in each step, knowing you're crafting experiences that touch hearts, open minds, and inspire souls. Here's to your success, your growth, and the remarkable legacy you're about to build. Here's to creating retreats that illuminate paths and guide people as they walk them. Let's embark on this continuous journey of transformation, impact, and legacy together.

Bonus Excerpt from my Best-Selling Book: 101 Ways Travel Improves Your Life

How Using a Travel Agent Improved My Travel Experiences

Expert Recommendations for Accommodations and Activities

Did you know there is a resort in Utah where you can stay in a yurt or a tiny house or a tree house? Neither did I. I wouldn't have even thought to look for that, but my travel agent knows I enjoy unique experiences and shared it with me. I spent half the trip in the yurt and half in a tiny house. The treehouses were all booked, but so cool!

But why would you book a trip with a travel agent when

you can go online and book an Airbnb with a cheap flight on Spirit and a pickup by Uber?

Because you only get so many vacation days, and they deserve to be the best!

Before you think to yourself that a travel agent is an extra expense, allow me to inform you that commission is built into every cruise, vacation package, most transportation (except domestic air), excursions, travel insurance, and many other interesting possibilities that a travel agent can share with you. **That means, that you are paying commission no matter if you book it or an expert books it for you.** That commission can go to a hard-working independent travel agent, or it can go to the corporate conglomerate that owns the supplier you book with, or the website you book on takes the cut. Of those three, which do you think will pick up the phone fastest when you need help?

When my mom's best friend went to college, she got a four-year degree to become a travel agent. Travel agents are professionals who are educated on travel, far more than you, make their living through your repeat business and referrals, so they are going to do everything to make your trip the most magical place on earth... even if you're not going to Disney. They offer expert recommendations for accommodations and activities that you probably don't know exist. Your agent will consider your preferences, budget, and desired experiences to provide curated suggestions that align with your interests and enhance your vacation.

Time and Stress Savings

I've been training travel agents on how to build 6-figure businesses since 2015. In that time, I've been introduced to over 100 travel supplier brands. And with all my knowledge nothing stresses me out like having to plan my own vacation. I don't want to take the time to compare all the suppliers and dig into the details and extras. You probably don't realize you don't either, because when people argue this point with me, I realize, "Oh, you don't want to do the boring monotonous stuff, you want to explore the fun stuff." By using a travel agent, it saves you time and reduces stress because by the time they come to you with three quotes for you to choose from, and you pick one... that's when you get to collaborate on the fun stuff! Let the travel agent handle the detailed research, booking, and logistics, so you can focus on enjoying your vacation without the hassle of extensive planning.

Expert Destination Knowledge

If you were getting married and there was only one bridal shop in town, so you had access to only those dresses or tuxes, but you had a wedding planner, who for no extra charge, had access for her clients to meet with 15 private designers, wouldn't you want the access? Travel agents not only have expert destination knowledge they also have access to suppliers who don't work with the public, and many of those are the ones that have super cool stuff, which is why they don't want to deal with the public. Agents also have firsthand experiences because they travel a lot and do site and ship inspections. Most have a network of clients and other travel agents with experiences, so if they haven't been where you want to go, they know someone who has. They stay current with their pulse on the news and the trends and with their up-to-date information will recommend the best destinations, accommodations, and activities for your specific preferences.

Customized Itineraries

I remember the day my parents were so excited to visit Notre-Dame. They even managed to convince my sister and me that we should be excited. We spent an entire day of our Paris vacation in line to see a Cathedral we spent about ten minutes in.

A good travel agent would never let that happen. You will have a "go around the line" ticket, so you can spend your ten minutes in the church and the rest of the day to see other sights that my family missed.

I won't put a price on the value of customized itineraries created by travel agents. I refer to them as your personal travel concierge because they tailor your vacation to your interests, ensuring that every aspect, from accommodations to sightseeing, aligns with your preferences and provides a unique life changing experience.

Access to Exclusive Deals and Upgrades

Along with access to the suppliers who aren't available to the public, travel agents have access to exclusive deals and upgrades that can enhance your vacation. Large travel agencies, like the one I work for, have deep industry connections spanning over 30 years and the booking power of our talented agents to negotiating special rates for our agents to offer which include amenities and discounts for their you. Travel agents will also ask if you are celebrating an occasion and will work with the suppliers to make sure you are celebrated properly. Will an online booking engine do that for you?

Assistance with Travel Documentation and Requirements

Did you know that if you are traveling out of the US your passport must be valid for six months beyond the date of your trip? I didn't. Until I tried to get on my first cruise ship, and they looked at my passport and told me my passport wasn't going to be valid... but on closer examination, I had made it by one day!!! And believe me, I had to argue for that one day. My stress level was through the roof!

Also on that first cruise, I was told to print out my luggage tags, but I figured, why print out luggage tags, I have really cute ones I bought on Amazon. Apparently, they weren't referring to the tags that have you contact information in case your bag is lost. There are specific tags that need to be printed out with your cabin information and more. Luckily, I know how to cry on cue, so the guy printed them out for me. I was off to a terrible start... but once on board I had a great time. That said, many cruise lines have pre-boarding deadlines for booking restaurants, shows and excursions that a travel agent will be aware of and keep you informed. The valuable assistance travel agents provide with travel documentation and requirements is unmatched. They will guide you through visa applications, passport renewals, travel insurance, and other necessary paperwork, ensuring a smooth and hassle-free travel experience.

Emergency Support and Travel Insurance

I don't care if you have the health of an elite athlete, the luck of a leprechaun and a family history of living to 103... always bet a travel insurance policy through a travel agent. I am not referring to the travel protection that airlines and other suppliers offer. Those are different and if you chose them over an insurance policy and something happens you will be sad, and mad, and it could be really bad!

I have heard too many horror stories from something as simple as living 15 minutes from the cruise port, but a fender bender made them so late that they missed the ship to a case of meningitis in Greece which put the guy out of commission for over a year in recovery (he did have insurance) to accidental deaths. My objective is not to make you fearful of travel. All those things can happen in everyday life. I simply want to impress upon you, that if you are making an investment that you can't afford to lose... protect it and yourself and your family.

Travel agents are also who you turn to for assistance during unexpected events, such as flight cancellations or medical emergencies or a runaway bride. I get way too confused when my flights are cancelled and don't really understand what's happening when the airline reps are rerouting everyone. So, I call my travel agent, she takes care of it, and I go find a funky-vibe BBQ joint in Austin airport, with a hot country singer on a corner stage... I know specific... because it really happened.

Insider Tips and Local Recommendations

When I ask a travel agent their favorite part of their job, they almost always say, "Making peoples' travel dreams come true." While I believe them, I imagine if I asked them their second favorite part, it would be traveling the world over to experience places so they can use their insider tips, local recommendations, hidden gems, off-the-beaten-path attractions, and authentic local experiences to enrich your vacation and help you discover the true essence of a destination.

Personalized Customer Service

I do a training for new travel agents called Demystifying Selling Travel. It has the most slides of any presentation I do. Why? Because your travel agent or travel advisor or as I like to refer to them, travel concierge's work starts from the minute you call them to guess when? Did you guess the minute you get home? Wrong. They never stop working for you. They prioritize your needs, provide ongoing support, and ensure that your travel arrangements are seamlessly coordinated, leaving you free to relax and enjoy your vacation. Then once you are home, they follow up, stay in touch, and think of you when something amazing gets their attention because they know you'll love it!

Post-Trip Support and Feedback

As I said, the travel agent's work does not end when your trip ends. They offer post-trip support and feedback. They'll want to hear about your travel experience, address any concerns, and use your valuable input to continuously improve their services and tailor future vacations to your preferences.

And remember what I said about their fees at the beginning of this chapter? Already built in, so commission is coming from the supplier not you. Some well-established travel agents do charge a service fee because they can. But if it's not in your budget you can find a spectacular travel agent who does not charge for their services.

Please, do yourself and your travel companions a solid, and use a good travel agent.